Samsung

MW01269263

1

(2 BOOKS IN 1)

(1)

Samsung Galaxy S21 Series Ultra 5G

The Complete Guide for Beginners to Master the New
Samsung Galaxy S21, S21 Plus & S21 Ultra 5G Including
Tips, Tricks and Troubleshooting Hacks

(2)

Samsung Galaxy S21 Camera Guide

The Complete User Manual for Beginners and Pro to Master
Professional Cinematic Videography and Photography Tips
and Tricks Using Samsung Galaxy S21, S21 Plus & Ultra

Curtis

Campbell

Disclaimer

The information in this book is based on personal experience and anecdotal evidence. Although the author has made every attempt to achieve an accuracy of the information gathered in this book, they make no representation or warranties concerning the accuracy or completeness of the contents of this book. Your circumstances may not be suited to some illustrations in this book.

The author disclaims any liability arising directly or indirectly from the use of this book. Readers are encouraged to seek Medical. Accounting, legal, or professional help when required.

This guide is for informational purposes only, and the author does not accept any responsibilities for any liabilities resulting from the use of this information. While every attempt has been made to verify the information provided here, the author cannot assume any responsibility for errors, inaccuracies or omission.

Printed in the United States of America

Table of Contents

Samsung Galaxy S21 Series Ultra 5G
The Complete Guide for Beginners to Master the New Samsung Galaxy S21, S21 Plus & S21 Ultra 5G Including Tips, Tricks and Troubleshooting Hacks

Samsung Galaxy S21 Camera Guide

The Complete User Manual for Beginners and Pro to Master Professional Cinematic Videography and Photography Tips and Tricks Using Samsung Galaxy S21, S21 Plus & Ultra

Samsung Galaxy S21 Series Ultra 5G

The Complete Guide for Beginners to Master the New
Samsung Galaxy S21, S21 Plus & S21 Ultra 5G Including
Tips, Tricks and Troubleshooting Hacks

INTRODUCTION

The Samsung Galaxy S21 series, the latest release of smartphones from Samsung, comes with some new features, ranging from sharper to so many other things. This book will give you a detailed guide on how to access the new features that Samsung has added to their devices. You will also learn about the camera features and how to use it to capture standard quality pictures, how to use the touch sensitivity, how to access the Samsung pay to carry out your daily transactions, use the parental guide to be able to monitor your kids' activities, change your screen resolution to suit your taste and so much more. At this book's conclusion, you will have the ability to navigate through the Samsung Galaxy S21 series device and enjoy it a lot better.

CHAPTER ONE

Comparison between Samsung Galaxy S21, S21 Plus, and S21 Ultra

We've got three new Samsung Galaxy, the S21, S21 Plus, and the S21 Ultra. The S21 is the smallest with a 6.2-inch display, the S21 Plus has a 6.7-inch display, and the S21 Ultra is the largest with a 6.8-inch display; all devices have small bezels with infinity or pie chart.

They all have Gorilla Glass protection, dynamic displays, and a maximum refresh rate of 120 hertz.

Although, the S21 and the S21 plus have some differences when placed side by side to the S21 Ultra. Below is a breakdown of what you would see.

Brightness: The brightness peak for the Galaxy S21 and S21 plus is about 1300 nits, but you'd get 1500 nits for the Galaxy S21 ultra, making it fantastic for viewing outdoors.

Resolution and display: The S21 and the S21 plus have a full HD plus resolution, the S21 Ultra has a quad HD plus resolution. This is the first time in many years that Samsung has gone back on the resolution on one of their S devices. So, it might be disappointing.

For the first time on a Samsung device, the S21 Ultra can support 120 hertz, with Quad HD plus resolution so that you can have that high resolution with that high refresh rate. Also, the S21 Ultra can switch between 11 to 120 hertz, making it a lot more efficient. The S21 Plus, however, can only switch between 48 and 120 hertz, so although you do have that adaptive refresh rate, it's not going to be as efficient as the S21 Ultra.

The final difference between the displays is something that you can see in the S21 and the S21 Plus, and it's that they have a flat display, whereas the S21 ultra has some curves on the side. This is something that Samsung has had for quite some time, but it looks like they are starting to move away from it. Some people prefer curved displays, while others prefer flat displays.

Design and the build: Samsung has updated their design, as you have the camera modules, kind of melting into the edges of the devices. You do have metal frames across all the devices. However, there are some key differences in terms of the material, the S21 plus and the S21 ultra have glass panels on the back, whereas the S21 has a plastic back, which Samsung likes to call 'plastic,' so it's not going to be as premium as the S21 plus and the S21 Ultra.

Again, this is going to come down to personal preference. Most people tend to put their device in a case, and if that is the case for you then, I don't think it's going to be a big deal because you're not going to be feeling it on your hands all the time.

But all three devices have an IP 68 water and dust resistance rating, which is always nice to have; all have a matte finish. Samsung has offered matte as well as glossy bags, but this time, you've got matte across the board, and you've got some color options. There are four color options available for the S21, three color options available for the S21 plus, and two color options available for the S21 Ultra. The flagship color for the S21 and the S21 Plus is the Phantom violet.

Cameras: For the cameras, you have more differences here, the camera module on the S21 ultra is much larger compared to the S21 and the S21 Plus, and that is because it has more cameras.

Looking at the S21 and the S21 Plus, they have the same cameras; there's a 10-megapixel selfie camera, and then you have a triple rear-facing camera setup.

There's a 12-megapixel ultra-wide camera, 12-megapixel primary camera, and a 64-megapixel telephoto zoom camera, which is going to give you three times optical zoom, the camera setup seems very similar to what they had on the S20 series, but the S21 ultra is what has a lot more of the improvements.

For the S21 ultra, there's a 14-megapixel selfie camera, and on the rear, you've got a few cameras, four cameras in total, as well as laser autofocus. Breaking these cameras down, your device's ultra-wide camera is 12-megapixel. Now, the key thing there is this camera has dual pixel autofocus which you don't have on the S21 and the S21 plus; this is going to allow you to use the ultra-wide camera as a macro camera, so when you get to objects around 10 centimeters or closer, it's going to switch the focus, and you'll be able to get some nice macro shots.

It uses the 12-megapixel ultra-wide camera sensor to focus closer; this is the same size as what we had for the S20 series, but it is an improved sensor, which is supposed to give you three times more dynamic range. It's also capable of capturing 12-bit raw files. It has optical image stabilization, and it uses the laser autofocus sensor to help it focus, which was a problem with the S20, so it's nice that Samsung has improved on it.

Also, you have two telephoto cameras; this is three times and 10 times two cameras, both have optical image stabilization and dual pixel autofocus. Samsung has said that they've also improved the zoom, so we do have a zoom lock feature, which kicks in when you are zooming in at the extremes; you can zoom up to 100 times.

There are also some improvements for videos, so firstly, you have 8K out of 24 frames per second, as they had with the S20 series; this goes across all the S21 series devices, but you now have 4k at 60 frames per second across all the cameras of the S21 Ultra.

You also have 4K up to 60 frames per second for the S21 and the S21 plus cameras, except for the telephoto camera. The telephoto camera does not have 4k at 60 frames per second; it only goes up to 4k at 30 frames per second.

Also, there are many new software features; one of them is the directive view, which will give you some advanced features for the cameras and allow you to preview the different lenses before switching to them. You've also got a single tape, 2.0, which uses multiple cameras to put together a piece for you. You also have a blogging view which will let you capture videos from the front and the rear-facing cameras at the same time.

Performance: The S21 series, as you've seen previously from Samsung, will vary depending on your region; some regions will be getting the Qualcomm Snapdragon 888 chipset, other regions will be getting Samsung's Exodus, 20, 120, 100 as was announced by Samsung company. It seems to have lots of improvements compared to the S20 series.

The S21 and the S21 plus comes with eight gigabytes of RAM, the S21 Ultra comes with 12 gigabytes of Ram, so it is going to be a multi-tasking beast for storage; we do have 128 and 256 gigabytes across all devices. The S21 Ultra comes with 512-gigabyte version storage. The S21 series does not have a micro SD card slot or IP. Because of the differences in speed, based on USPS 3.1 storage and even some of the fastest micro SD card slots.

Software: All the devices come with Android 11 out of the box and a brand new fingerprint sensor. It has the Qualcomm 3D Sonic sensor Generation Two; this is 1.7

times larger than the previous generation and 50% faster.

The S21 Plus and the S 21 Ultra also have ultra-wideband technology, and this will allow a few things as Samsung have talked about using the devices as a digital touchless key for your car, there is improved Android Auto. There's also integration with smart things from Samsung, so you'll be able to get some smart tags to be able to locate things much easier. The S21 Ultra also comes with some unique features which you won't get on the S21 and the S21 plus.

Firstly, you do have hyper-fast WiFi 6, which can give you up to four times fast WiFi speeds, and for the S21 ultra, it has support for the S Pen; this is the first time you've got S Pen support on a Galaxy S device. This isn't going to be included in your purchase; it's an accessory that's sold separately bundled with a case because there is no space in the S21 Ultra for the S Pen like you have on the Note series.

Others: Based on the size of the devices, of course, the S21 has the smallest battery of 4000 milliamps. The S21 Plus has a 4800 milliamp battery, and the S21 ultra with the biggest 5000 milliamp battery. All devices support up to 25-watt fast charging of up to 15 watts and wireless charging. They also have reverse wireless charging where you can use the devices to charge some galaxy buds or another device altogether. But none of the devices come with a charger or earphones out of the box.

The S21 series is priced lower quite a bit lower compared to the S20 series. So, the Samsung Galaxy S21 starts at $800 or 769 pounds the S21 plus comes in at $1,000 or 950 pounds. S21 ultra, at $13100 or €11150.

Power up Your Device

If you want to switch on your Samsung Galaxy S21 series, all you have to do is to click and hold the Power button until you see the Samsung logo on the screen. So, right there on the right edge, click and hold. Keep holding. Now, release and wait for the phone to turn on.

How To Locate Your Sim Tray And Insert Your SIM Card

You will need the SIM ejector which is inside the box. The SIM tray is located on the bottom side of the device. When you take it out, you have space for two different SIM cards in there. So you can place one SIM card on either side with a chip facing outward. And that's all it takes to insert your SIM card.

Starting Up Your Device

Now, when you boot it up for the first time, you'll be presented with what to see, which is the welcome screen, and all languages to choose from, similar to how Apple does it. From there, tap on the blue button and select your language, then you click on **Next** and connect to a mobile network. This page is strictly for SIM cards, you can insert your SIM card if you've not done it, or you can do that later on, but nothing will change.

On the next page, you have the fueling items to review. You need to agree to the End User License Agreement but you don't have to agree to anything else apart from that, so don't select anything else there and click on next.

On the next page, you have the WiFi network. You can connect to WiFi if you have one near you. If you don't, then don't worry; you can skip it. The only downside of skipping it is the date and time won't be set automatically based on the connection. Also, you won't have the ability to connect to a Google account throughout the setup. So, once you connect to WiFi or insert a SIM card with a mobile network, you can do that through the settings by going to **settings and accounts,** and then it will come up from there.

You can restart your device from an old backup from the settings, click on **next** if you're setting it up as new, and click on **don't copy.** As you progress, you see Google services. There's a couple of different services; you have location scanning and send user and diagnostic data.

You can go briefly over all three of the location and GPS tracking, which Google Maps commonly use, so it gives you a correct route to your destination when you're using the navigation of your car, for instance.

Also, you have the scanning that allows the phone to scan for signals like Bluetooth devices and WiFi connections. The sending of the user and diagnostic data and self-explanatory gathers data on using the device to send it to Google.

Now, if you don't want any of those, you can disable all of them from the "Thanks page," where you can set protection toward your device. You can choose face recognition or fingerprint which will require you to set a pattern or password. You will not be able to use the only fingerprint with face recognition or face recognition with a fingerprint because if something happens to you, either the finger or the face gets busted, you can be locked out of your phone. So that's why there are three physical ways of unlocking the device with a pattern. Draw the pattern, redraw the same pattern, and confirm, and that will automatically set the pattern.

Find my mobile or find my device; Samsung pass is a simple and secure way to signup and upgrade, like allowing you to store passwords on your Google account and then using your fingerprint to unlock them.

CHAPTER TWO

SmartSwitch Data Transfer

STEP: 1 You need to turn on the settings of the Smart switch on the Galaxy S21.

STEP: 2 Tap on "Sync"

STEP: 3 Select "WiFi or Cellular" and select "Data."

STEP: 4 Enter your SSID or password and tap "OK."

STEP: 5 Choose your data plan and name your phone

STEP: 6 You will be asked to select a preferred language

STEP: 7 You will be shown a list of data subscription services that can be used. You need to select the one that suits you and tap on "save."

STEP: 8 If you want to add another data subscription, click on "Edit" and choose from the list

STEP: 9 Now, turn on data sharing on your smartphone, click on "Sync," and select your data plan.

STEP: 10 You will be asked to wait; after a while the data will be transferred to the Galaxy S21

You can use this feature even if you do not have a mobile data plan, but remember that you will only be able to connect to WiFi.

Google Account Set Up

Once your Google account is synced to your Galaxy S21, you will be able to use the Google Assistant and perform most actions like search the web or send emails.

Step 1: Tap on the Menu icon in the top left corner

Step 2: Go to Settings> Account

Step 3: Select Google Account> Sync phone

Step 4: Check 'Sync now.'

Step 5: Once done, you can use your new Samsung Galaxy S21 with the help of Google Assistant.

Setting Up Your Security System And Password

As the number of phone users increases day by day, security threat has become serious and you might be worried about your phone's privacy. Therefore, to prevent any unauthorized access to your phone, there is the option to set up a security feature. This feature is very easy to use and also allows you to configure the privacy and security settings.

Following the below-mentioned steps can be used to set up a security system on your Samsung S21 plus

STEP 1.

First of all, you need to make sure that the phone has at least a 30% battery charge. For this, select the emergency mode and hold the power button on the phone until you get to a familiar screen.

STEP 2.

You need to hold the power button and volume down buttons together to select the emergency mode. Select the 'Emergency rescue' option to turn off the feature.

STEP 3.

After this, there is another mode that you need to set. Now, you have to select the 'Encryption' option.

STEP 4.

The security option will appear on the screen. Here you need to select the 'Log in Settings' option, and if you do not have to enter your social media accounts, you can skip the step. If you want to set up a Google account, you need to enter the account information.

STEP 5.

Now, set up the password for the security feature. You need to enter the password when you enter the phone in emergency mode. After you have set up the password, tap on the 'Continue' option; after this, there is the option to 'Log out,' which you need to tap on.

How To Log In Or Create A Samsung Account

STEP 1

Launch **Settings app.** Scroll down to the main settings menu to Account options, then Select Sign In or Sign Up, Select Sign In if you have a Samsung Account, and choose to create a new account if you don't have an account.

STEP 2

Tapping "Create new account" in the "Sign In" menu will take you to a new screen with four options. The first option is similar to that of the "Create account" in the Wallet app. The second is similar to the service provider authentication page, the third is an affiliate account creation, and the fourth is a Live ID account creation. The option closest to the last one is what you are looking for.

STEP 3

The "Create account" screen will prompt you to enter the email address, password, and security question. You can also choose a verification method to use for the account so that you will be presented with one last screen. Enter the email address associated with the Samsung account and enter the password. The verification method is the same as that of the Samsung Pay account, and it is entered in the same form.

STEP 4

You will now be presented with an authorization URL. Now, enter the Access Key, and Security Code displayed at the top of the screen, tap the "Yes" button, and tap on the proceed button. Congratulations, you have created a Samsung account!

CHAPTER THREE

Accessing All Apps And Downloading Apps On Playstore

Accessing all apps

To access the apps on your device, launch your home screen; from the home screen, swipe up your device, it will bring you to all the apps on your device in alphabetical order.

Downloading Apps

Step 1: Go to the google play store and download it. The search button will be on the left of the app store.

Step 2: Now, you will see your choice apps you can choose them to download and install.

Step 3: Once you have downloaded the apps, you can use them.

How To Manage Your Home Screen

The Samsung Galaxy S21 series all have a super AMOLED display with an FHD resolution and Corning Gorilla Glass protection. The home screen gives a transparent look so that you can see the various widgets and applications easily. You can configure it in a few steps.

Turn off the dark theme: If you are using a dark theme on your home screen, then you will want to disable it for performance reasons. To toggle on and off the dark theme, press and hold the option for "Theme" and drag the toggle to the 'Off' position.

Replace the Clock Icon: To add a clock icon to the home screen, tap on Settings. Add a clock icon with the text clock to add a clock to the home screen, then tap on Done.

Add icon: To add a custom app icon to the home screen, tap on Settings, then on Home Screen, tap on Add Icon, and choose the desired app. Then tap on Done.

Take all the app icons to the left: The home screen is divided into two halves. There's a left side with the apps, and the right side has the widgets and the clock. So how can you change the left side to show all the app icons instead of the widgets? You need to drag the app icons to the left to get them aligned with the other app icons on the right. There are no app icons on the right side, so this might look strange to you. If you don't like this, you can always remove all the app icons on the right and reorder them.

Hide the grid: If you don't like the home screen's square grid layout, you can add the grid to the left or right side by dragging the grid line. If you do this, then the navigation bar on top will appear on the left.

Adjust the size of the navigation bar: To adjust the size of the navigation bar, tap on the three vertical dots in the navigation bar, then select the Size option from the menu. The minimum and maximum sizes of the navigation bar will be shown.

Uninstall apps: You can uninstall apps by opening the app drawer and tapping on the three vertical dots at the top, then tap on 'Uninstall apps.'

Select the apps you want to remove, then tap on 'Done.'

Minimize widgets: If you want to minimize all the widgets on the home screen, tap on the three vertical dots at the top, then tap on the 'Minimize option.' After minimizing all the widgets, then tap on the 'Done button.'

Managing Your Contact

The basic way of managing your contact on the Samsung Galaxy S21 series is not limited to users, anyone can use this app to manage their contacts. They can manage their contacts by dragging and dropping the address book to the side so that you can access the contacts easily.

You can limit the number of contacts you want to display by using a filter. You can choose "Type & color" to make your phone look beautiful.

The basic option is "Drag & drop" where you drag and drop your contacts to the contact list, use the two-finger swipe to resize the contacts, or drag and drop your text. You can also drag and drop from inside any app to add contacts.

The best thing about using this app is that it not only lets you view your contact information but it also shows a full picture of who you are talking to. It also allows you to create new contacts like on a normal phone. You can also check the number of the person that you are talking to. This app allows you to create as many groups as you want.

There are also a few features that Samsung Galaxy S21 users can benefit from:

It displays the full pictures of the people you are talking to on a full screen.

You can manage your email address if you are using Android email services such as Gmail, Yahoo, Outlook, etc. It enables you to manage your Facebook account information (keyboard shortcut to open Facebook and switch accounts to manage existing and new contacts

CHAPTER FOUR

Setting Up Your WiFi Connection

Step 1

First, tap on the Home key to take you back to your home screen, and then swipe down at a tab to open up the Quick Settings panel.

Step 2

Next, you're going to tap on the Settings icon. In there, tap on connections then tap on WiFi. Once WiFi is switched on, wait for your device to scan for available networks.

Step 3

Now, on the network that you would like to connect to, you need to put in the network password once you tap on the network.

Step 4

After you have put in the password, tap on the connect button. And that will allow you to connect to your WiFi router. And that's it, so wait for it to check the quality of your internet connections. Once it is connected, you should see the signal at the top of your screen on the status bar.

Step 5

The WiFi icon gives you an indication that you are now connected to WiFi. If you are seeing a WiFi icon with an exclamation mark, that is an indicator that you are connected to WiFi, but you are having issues accessing the internet.

Setting Up Your E-SIM

Step 1

First, go back to your home screen by tapping on the Home key. From there, swipe down on top and tap on the Settings icon in settings, tap on connections, then go down and tap on SIM card manager.

Step 2

Now, tap on **add mobile plan.** You can see at the top is your physical SIM card; this is the SIM card that you inserted into the SIM slot. The device also supports other SIMs which makes the device HQ Sim. Tap on the "Add mobile plan," and there it will try to search to see if there is a plan attached to the phone already. If not, you can tap on the scan carrier QR code. As you can see, if you tried to search again, it will try to attempt the search; if it doesn't find anything, it will come back with no plans found so that you can tap on scan a QR code.

Step 3

Now, this allows you to use the camera to scan the QR code that comes with your E-SIM package. When you go to your network carrier, you can ask them for an E-SIM. They normally give out a package that also has an activation card or a QR code attached to the package. Once you're home with your package, use your phone camera to scan for the QR code.

Step 4

From there, you can set up your E-SIM. If you do not have a QR code on the package, there should be some kind of activation code that you could put in.

After putting in the activation code, you can connect and set up your E-SIM.

Setting Up All Your Sounds And Ringtones

Samsung has a few settings in the 'Advanced Sounds & Ringtone' and 'Sounds & notification' settings on your phone. Before you go on with the steps on setting up sound and ringtones on your Samsung Galaxy S21, you should know that you can set up certain sounds and ringtones only on specific contacts in your phone, and in most cases, not all the contacts have that specific sound or ringtone. Also, Samsung allows you to add up to 300 distinct sounds and ringtones to your phone.

As per Samsung, here are the steps you can take to set up sound and ringtones on your Samsung Galaxy S21 series:

Open the Settings.

Select 'Sound & notification.'

Scroll down and select 'Advanced Sounds & Ringtone.'

Scroll down to 'Alarm' and click on it.

Select the number of sounds to be included in your Steps on how to set up sounds and ringtones o your device... From this setting, you will be able to customize any of your sounds and you can as well put off the sound.

Using Notification To Manage How Your Device Notifies You

Go to Settings -> Notification. Here you can set up sound control for every notification.

How to turn off sound?

Go to Settings -> Sound -> No sound.

How to enable sound for notifications?

Go to Settings -> Sound -> Automatically enable sound for notifications.

CHAPTER FIVE

Display Set-Up

Talking about the display setting, it appears to be a luxurious one. The Samsung Galaxy S21 series have the following settings for dsisplay settings: Dynamic brightness, Brightness temperature, brightness adjustment, Brightness control, Brightness control at power saving, Dimming, 'Always on display,' Multi-window and Quick Reply.

Dynamic brightness – it changes the brightness according to your environment lighting condition. You can set different levels of brightness for each app. For example, you can set it to 50% brightness when you are outdoors.

Brightness temperature – this is set as per your choice. You can set it from 0 to 250; for that you need to click on 'Brightness control at power saving.'

Brightness adjustment – you can set this up according to your preference. Here it is recommended to set it at a high level.

Brightness control at power saving – It can be set to -20 degrees Fahrenheit or 20 degrees Celsius. This will automatically turn the brightness down. It will turn on automatically when your phone is plugged into a power source.

Dimming – this will adjust the brightness of the screen based on your preference. It can be set according to your liking.

Brightness control at power saving – Here, you can set it according to your preference; for that you need to click on 'Brightness control at power saving.'

Always on display – This is an eye-catching feature. It adds a screen light on the screen with a green color that will turn on and turn off. You need to activate this by clicking on 'Always-on display.' This turns the screen 'off' when not in use and can be enabled by clicking on 'always-on display.'

Quick Reply – You can use the action by making the screen appear instantly when you receive a message from the supported application. You need to click on the 'quick reply' button which is located at the top right corner. Now, click on 'remind me later' to see the list of apps. From the list, you select the message you want to see then click on 'quick reply,' and all the application icons will appear in a small window, which will reply to them.

Using Easy Mode

There is a new mode on Samsung Galaxy S21 phones to optimize performance and multitasking. The phones are capable of offering two panels on the display screen for a better user experience.

But sometimes, multitasking can get cumbersome due to the number of notifications, especially with group calls. It's time to fix this issue as now you can switch to easy mode on your Samsung Galaxy S21 to get rid of the annoying notification.

Here's how to use easy mode on Samsung Galaxy S21 series:

Step 1: Go to the Settings -> Click on the More menu and select advanced mode.

Step 2: Now, tap on the option of easy mode; this will activate it instantly.

Step 3: Select a profile, then long-press the shortcut key.

Step 4: Tap on the option and select OK. It's that simple.

You can also enable the 'Do not Disturb' option.

Using And Setting Up The Edge Panel Function

To install the new edge panel feature, you have to head over to Settings -> Advanced features -> Edge Panel and install the new Edge panel widget.

After installing it, you can find this widget in the list of panels.

Mail: Swipe from right to left to see messages. Swipe from right to left to remove them.

Messages: Swipe from right to left to view unread messages. You can delete or reply to messages when you swipe from right to left.

Music: Access the music playlist by swiping from right to left. Delete or listen to a preview by swiping from right to left. Access the new music player by swiping from right to left.

Samsung Health: Access health and fitness information swiping from right to left. Switch off the tracking mode by swiping from right to left.

Navigation Bar Management

If you are a fan of the navigation bar of Samsung Galaxy S21, you should know that the new setting will allow users to customize the interface.

Do note that the only way to disable the navigation bar from the Samsung Galaxy S21 is to go into the settings menu and check the new "Display & touch" option from the accessibility options. By turning on the slider and pressing "Appearance & touch," you can customize the navigation bar for better performance.

Having said that, you can also choose to disable the icon, which lets you use the navigation bar. For instance, if you want to disable the search bar at the bottom of the navigation bar, then you can do so from the accessibility menu.

However, if you do so, you will lose out on the accessibility options that are useful for those who need it the most.

The display & touch Setting on the Samsung Galaxy S21 setting bar, after a close inspection, it is easy to see that there are three options available under this new "Display & touch" option on Galaxy S21 series. You can go ahead and make any changes that you like if you face issues after making changes. The option also reveals the transparency of the navigation bar along with the navigation bar settings.

Using Touch Sensitivity

Touch sensitivity
Increase the touch sensitivity of the screen for use with screen protectors.

What is touch sensitivity?

Touch sensitivity means the ability to provide a good user experience on a touch screen phone. Compared to a button, which does not need the side-mounted buttons, the experience can be a little improved.

After the user changes the capacitive touch sensitivity settings of the Galaxy S21 Plus, the index finger's touch sensitivity is up to five times more accurate. This means that touch sensitivity can be adjusted for different modes like browser (quick swipe) and game (power button). Users can also use software and hardware touch sensors to further improve the touch experience on the Galaxy S21 series.

Can I lock touch sensitivity?

Yes, you can even adjust touch sensitivity for specific touch modes on the Galaxy S21. For instance, there are modes to snap images quickly in the Samsung Camera app, panorama mode, slow motion, time-lapse, and video, etc. You can increase or decrease the touch sensitivity in these modes to enable your touch experience better.

To turn on the new feature, you need to swipe from left to right on the top left corner of the screen. This would activate the feature then all you need to do is touch the screen gently and get a confirmation message. You can do this up to five times in a row and each time, the screen will be quieter and this is equivalent to turning off the touch sensitivity feature.

CHAPTER SIX

Setting Up Wallpapers And Themes

Go to your phone's gallery and search for "Galaxy S21 wallpaper." Tap on the wallpaper that you want to change and hold your device steady. Tap on the menu icon and Select 'wallpaper.' Choose "Wallpapers and themes" from the "Choose wallpaper and backgrounds" section. Change the color and tap on the Home button, and then select "Lock home screen." Enjoy your new wallpaper!

How to create customized UI themes

You can use a custom-made UI theme to completely change your Samsung Galaxy S21 series's look and feel. Go to your phone's settings, select themes, and then select "Create a new custom theme" from the options.

Here's a guide on how to create a custom theme

Go to Settings > Widgets & Notifications > Samsung theme picker > Set your theme! Select your preferred skin or theme. If the theme has colors, select the color of the skin to set the new color for the lock screen.

How To Change The Home Screen

Samsung Galaxy S21 has a native home screen configuration from Samsung. It is similar to other Samsung devices, except that it has a set of on-screen buttons and icons, and you can easily hide or even change the layout if you don't like it. Let's learn how you can change the home screen layout on Galaxy S21 series.

If you do not like the layout, here is how you can change it:

Go to Settings>> Screen calibration>> Screen layout. Tap on Customize layout. Here you can change the layout as follows:

'No icon' can be selected.

One can also choose the images to be displayed on the home screen. Choose the wallpaper from the Gallery and select image(s) from there. The selected image will appear in the list of thumbnails on the Home Screens layout screen. Tap on the select image(s) to select the images to use as a Home Screen icon

Don't like the order of the home screens? You can arrange them differently. In the Customization section, tap on the Updater option. Tap on Next. The Updater will sort out the Home Screens in a different order, and then you can select the order of home screens on the Home Screens layout screen.

How To Set Up Google Protect

Google protect was first released in August 2015, so you might not know it is already available for Samsung users on Android smartphones. So here's the guide on how to install the application on Samsung Galaxy S21 smartphones.

What is google protect?

On its website, the program says: "With Google Protect, you can back up your data, get virus protection, secure your search history and keep your apps safe." When you install it, you get three free months. But after the given time limit, you can get a pro version that will give you unlimited backup data and even secure your browser history.

For installation on Samsung phones, follow these simple steps:

1. Open the settings app Tap on Google Now (bottom right corner)

2. Scroll down and tap on Apps, select Google icon to get to Settings

3. Scroll down and tap on security. Now, select 'Google protect' to start using it; you might need to download it from the Google Play Store for Samsung phones. In the app, you can select your devices and even create backups via ADB. In case of any problems, users can contact Google Protection Support.

Using Secure Folder

Samsung Galaxy S21 series comes with a Secure Folder, and it can be accessed from the Applications folder. It can be added manually or set as a default application to an installed application.

To access this option, go to Settings –> Advanced features –> Security & lock screen options and add Secure Folder application.

Secure Folder allows you to protect sensitive content on the device by locking it. If the application cannot access it in the Secure Folder, it won't be able to view or change it.

After adding, select the folder, then tap on the "Lock/Unlock" button to turn it on or off.

If you don't want to lock the application, then you can long-press on the icon, and "Recents" and "Lock/Unlock" options will be shown.

Using Private Share

STEP 1

Open Settings and select 'Assist,' and there will be several options, including 'Accessibility,' 'Assist switch,' 'Accessory Type,' and 'Advanced Accessory,' and it will ask you to use your fingerprint to unlock.

STEP 2

Confirm the fingerprint and then turn on security. Under "Accessory Type" use Accessory Share. There you can see that you can directly share your device screen or photo with any other device or individual using the Bluetooth feature. You can also share any files like .doc, .pdf, .jpg or .xls. So, it saves time in transferring files using Bluetooth.

CHAPTER SEVEN

Using Privacy Settings To Control Apps That Can Access Your Device

Your device has a dedicated privacy mode where you can hide pictures, videos, contacts, and even settings.

By doing so, you can set it so that no one but you can see your picture gallery, text messages, contacts, and even the Facebook or Twitter account you set up for your phone. It also allows you to disable or edit what certain apps can access, such as contacts.

How to enable privacy mode

STEP 1: Tap on the Menu button from the home screen.

STEP 2: Tap on Settings.

STEP 3: Scroll down to Privacy Mode.

STEP 4: Tap on 'Enable.'

When the screen goes black, a big white triangle will appear at the top of the screen. A circular white dot will appear in the top-right corner. The phone will then be unlisted.

Accessing The Location Set-Up

Step 1: Open the Phone application on your device.

Step 2: Select the Gear icon on the left side of the screen.

Step 3: Select the Settings option and then select Location.

Step 4: Now tap on 'location set up' and enable the feature.

Step 5: Now, tap on the 'makeup and security' option and then enable the features.

Step 6: Restart your phone, and you are done.

Accessing The Advanced Feature Of Google Backup

STEP 1

First of all, you should turn on your phone. Then search google on your phone to download and install the Backup Manager app.

STEP 2

After downloading, open the app and wait until it is ready to be installed. While installing the app, don't touch any option as it has something to do with data loss.

STEP 3

Now, go to the Settings app on your phone and tap on the Backup & reset option. Once the option turns on, you will be able to access the advanced option.

STEP 4

You need to select the Backup option. Then tap on "Create a backup." Finally, confirm it. After that, you will be able to access the backup of data that was backed up. You can choose the file that you wish to backup and finally click on the "Done" button.

How To Connect Your Device To Windows Computer

Samsung has an ultra HD display, and this device can be connected to a Windows computer through a USB cable. Here, I am sharing the steps you should follow to connect the Samsung Galaxy S21 series with a windows computer.

Step 1: Connect USB cable with your Samsung Galaxy S21. Now, plug it on to your Windows computer.

Step 2: Click on the network icon in your taskbar and click on "connect to wireless networks," you will get some network options such as un-tether, tethering, etc

Step 3: Click on your home WiFi network name if you are using your mobile phone number like 1234567890 for the wiFi network.

Step 4: Find your wireless network name, type the mobile number, click connect, and voila! You will see the network name like a wireless network in your taskbar.

And that's It. You can now use your Samsung Galaxy device on your Windows computer.

Using Samsung Dex With A Computer

STEP 1

Once you turn on the phone, open the Odin command tool. Make sure you are connected to your PC via LAN cable to download and install the correct Odin files needed to modify the phone files.

STEP 2

Ensure that your device is not charged. You can turn it off by holding down the power key until the phone reboots. After this, you will enter a recovery mode.

STEP 3

Enable USB Debugging. You will see a notification in the bottom right corner. In case you are not getting any notification, go to Settings → Developer Options → USB Debugging.

STEP 4

Now connect your Samsung phone to your PC. After this, select 'Creative player' and 'Odin flashing tool.' On the ODIN screen, select the firmware file to flash. It looks like this (Samsung Galaxy S21F550SFSFXX_3EVJRV08_EN-US_13MB.zip).

STEP 5

Then, you will be asked to select a recovery option. Select 'install custom recoveries.' Select the .zip file, and click on the 'yes' button to proceed. Now, you will be asked to set up a password for your device.

STEP 6

Select the wipe data/factory reset option. Then, select the 'Wipe data/factory reset' button again.

Wait until the process is complete, then wait until you get the device back on your PC.

STEP 7

Once you receive the data file on your computer, you can launch it using Odin. This is when you will see that data is lost, and only the boot animation and set of directories are present on your phone. Make sure you have backed up all the important data of your phone before doing this, so you don't lose any of your stuff if something goes wrong.

Using Samsung Pay

To make Samsung pay work, open the notification bar and tap on 'Samsung Pay.' Once this is done, it will open a payment gateway that allows you to use Samsung pay, like how you can pay using mobile wallets. In this case, you can pay at any of Samsung's partner stores using your debit and credit card. If you don't have a debit card and your credit card is blocked, you can still use your IC or American Express card. All you have to do is to activate Samsung Pay on the phone and scan your card or swipe your credit card. You will get a notification when Samsung pay has been added to the account.

Here's how to use Samsung Pay

Step 1: Go to the Samsung app store and download the Samsung Pay app.

Step 2: Once this is done, open the app, and you will be asked to create a Samsung Pay card.

Step 3: You can link your IC or American Express card to Samsung Pay.

Step 4: Then, enter your credentials, and you are all set.

On the Samsung Pay feature page, you will see a list of the supported banks and cards along with details. The process to add a card is very simple. You can also add multiple cards to Samsung Pay.

Also, if you want to make payments to government websites and services, you can do that using Samsung pay. You can also use your debit and credit cards with Samsung Pay to make payments using internet banking services.

Using Samsung Health

Samsung Galaxy S21 series comes with a Samsung health app where you can monitor your body's physical activity with a fitness tracker. It uses a proprietary heart rate sensor, GPS, and accelerometer to track your daily movement and calories burnt. Samsung also provides sleep apnea detection and also indicates the patterns to improve your breathing quality.

The sensor located on the back of the device measures heart rate, blood oxygen levels, and overall health. Samsung Health also includes a heat sensor to alert users when they are not being active.

You can download the app from the Galaxy Apps store. Once downloaded, you can set up the Health app by creating an account, adding some data, and choosing a goal.

In Samsung Health, search by Exercise type. Select the type you are interested in, and it'll display more details for your exercise, including how to set up the exercise.

Create a Google account, so you can easily log in with it. If you don't have one already, create one.

- Select Exercise type – there are lots of options to choose from. Set it up how you want it – cardio, weights, etc.
- Select the option you want, and it'll give you step-by-step exercise instructions on how to do the exercise. Click on the camera icon to record.

- Enter your workout time which will then be visible on your phone in the Samsung Health app.
- View your workout history and workout status.

You can update information such as date of birth or change your BMI with the 'My Profile' option on the 'My Exercise' Record screen.

Start, stop, and pause workouts.

Hover on the camera icon on the right to select the manual recording button.

View phone notifications.

There is a clip available at the end of the video which you can download by clicking on it. Also, your selected exercise's email address will be emailed and added automatically in the "Data" section of Samsung Health.

CHAPTER EIGHT

Using Motions And Gestures

Other than all these good specs, one more thing you can look forward to is its touchscreen and motion control features that it can offer you.

For this purpose, first, you need to download and install the Google Mobile Services from the Play Store, though if you haven't installed them, go to Google and install them. Once they are installed, open it and search for the following apps:

Phone

Assistant

Google Search

Now, go to the Phone app and tap on the three dots (three vertical dots) on the top right corner and then tap on the 'open settings' menu option and then tap on 'general.' Now, tap on 'motion control' option and then tap on the three dots on the top right corner and then tap on the gestures option. Now, tap on gestures, then tap on circle, then tap on 'press and hold.'

On that screen, enter your password, and voila! Now, turn on the phone, tap on the home button and that's how you set up the gestures and motion control on this phone.

If you are wondering what the gestures and motion control options are, you can know that they can be turned off. To uncheck this option, go to the main settings menu option and then go to 'general' and tap on the three dots and then tap on the gestures option. Now, tap on 'uncheck the options', and it's gone.

Using S-Pen

Samsung Galaxy S21 series has improved with the Smart Select feature that allows users to take notes similarly as you would take notes on a tablet. It allows the user to take photos, make a video, jot down notes, and much more. The features available for Galaxy S21 smartphones include Smart Select, Action Memo, and AutoSave.

To make use of the Samsung S-Pen on Galaxy S21 series, you will have to launch the dedicated S-Pen application from the preinstalled Galaxy Apps store.

Once you open the app, you will see a new section on the top-left corner of the screen, which will showcase 'What's New.' If the feature is enabled, the icon will turn into an S-Pen icon and be swiped left to the right to enable the feature. You can now swipe on the icon to activate the Note-style features.

The S-Pen can do more than taking notes as you can also use it to add text to your photos. Now, you can also write on the photo and edit the image after the writing. You can directly touch the icon in the photo and tap on the 'Edit text' option. From there, you can tap on the word 'Quick Action' option to take the edit as well as share the image. You can either select the word that you want to have edited, or you can start writing a message as well.

The app supports both the translate and translate-to-voice feature as well, which will convert the text to any other language using your S-Pen, and you can switch back to English. For example, after you have shared the translated text. The ability to translate the text on the Galaxy S21 smartphones makes the device one of the best android options to use with your friends or colleagues.

Setting Up Digital Wellbeing And Parental Control

Samsung Galaxy S21 series' new child protection features make it easy for parents to understand and monitor their children's online behavior and ensure that their children are safe and happy online.

The device comes with a new SNS notifications feature, which can identify any unauthorized calls or SMS, and the phone will automatically send an OTP for users to approve.

It also comes with an SOS feature, which allows users to make emergency calls from any location on the device without requiring a cell network connection. Once activated, this feature can be used in an emergency.

Taking some time out from your smartphone to get to sleep, watch a film, or relax can be helpful. You may want to use the TV app on Samsung Galaxy S21 to avoid accidentally checking Facebook on the TV.

You can start or stop the TV watching activity at any time. The Samsung TV also has a separate viewing mode that will stop the TV's screen from lighting up or disturbing the kids. You can toggle this off or on, should you need to.

You can also use Airplane mode to prevent WiFi and mobile data signals from getting through, making sure the children are not able to contact the outside world. They can also navigate to the web browser and play games, although it's worth noting that these apps are not kid-safe.

CHAPTER NINE

Managing Your Battery Storage

Don't watch videos, play games, download large files, or play online multiplayer games; it will drain the battery rapidly, and once that happens, you'll get less battery life.

Turn off Auto Call Blocker in Samsung Galaxy S21 series

If you're not getting your calls or message so far, turn off the Auto Call Blocker on your Samsung Galaxy S21. This will decrease the chances of you being in this unfortunate situation.

Use Gaming Mode on Samsung Galaxy S21 plus

Using Gaming Mode on Samsung Galaxy S21 will decrease your device's battery usage and boost the performance of your device.

If you want to get more battery life, then just follow this tip.

Take a small break for your Samsung Galaxy S21 series to sleep

Set the alarm on your Samsung Galaxy S21, and set an extended power-saving mode. Sleep as long as you can, and your phone will need the least energy to survive.

The thing is, if you do this regularly, you'll be shocked how much battery life you'll get in a day.

Optimizing Your Device

Create a RAM disk in Device Manager with 12 GB Memory Space; 10 GB is enough. Tap on "Reboot" on the Boot screen

Install the Samsung Updater program; you will get an extra 512 MB of RAM on your device

Now, after installing the above-mentioned Samsung Updater program, you will get more RAM for the same storage; this will allow you to run all your heavy applications on your device without any hiccups.

We will give you the exact method of removing all unwanted applications and cache in the following steps:

Go to settings, select device maintenance, select storage, and delete all unnecessary apps cache.

After removing cache and drivers, it will increase the storage space in your device, and you will no more get the root access problem.

Managing Your Apps Cache And Data

Samsung devices come with file explorer which is quite useful for finding files on the internal memory or memory card. One of the hidden features is that Samsung doesn't limit users to delete the content on the SD card after the phone was purchased. The device also includes a feature called cache, which is used to retain user data and applications for a specified time.

Once you install a game app, there will be a cache on your device, and this cache is used to keep some things that you use frequently. The cache allows you to save the apps that you want to get back to the home screen quickly. The cache is a type of virtual memory, and it is downloaded in the RAM; this virtual memory can be removed from the phone at any time. The operating system also uses the cache to recover your apps when the device is not being used for a few seconds.

It stays even when you are not using your phone; it is not used for web browsing, charging the device, etc.

How to remove the cache from your device

Step 1: Press and hold Volume up and Home buttons at the same time for few seconds.

Step 2: After some time, you will see a storage manager running on the phone; press the power button to exit the device manager.

Step 3: You will now see an option for clearing cache on the Samsung Galaxy S21 series, select it and press the Power button to apply the update. After few seconds, the cache will be removed.

Step 4: After the cache has been removed, you will see that the device has two hidden apps on the Home screen. To see these apps, you have to find the hidden content on the SD card of the phone, tap on it and select the Clear cache button. You can check out some more hidden features of the Samsung Galaxy S21 series.

CHAPTER TEN

Setting Up Text To Speech

Step 1

Open Galaxy Apps by going to the Home screen, tap on Apps from the menu bar, then tap on App Settings. Tap on Samsung Accessibility > Service.

Step 2

If you have already enabled Voice Recognition and Content Pause, tap on the toggle next to Smart Voice to the Off position. Press the Return/Back button to return to the home screen and select the Voice over section.

Step 3

Curtis Campbell

Once you tap on the toggle next to VoiceOver, tap on the application toggle to enable it. Swipe down from the top right corner and select the Menu option in the notification bar to navigate through the Samsung Apps.

Step 4

You will then be able to select the VoiceOver option from the list of audio applications you have already enabled. Once you find the one you want to use, tap on the toggle to activate it.

Setting Up Your Date And Time

Step 1: Locate the Lock Screen and then swipe up from the bottom right corner to open the menu, showing the clock and date.

Step 2: Tap on the "Set Date," Time and Date button.

Step 3: Select a selected date and time.

82

Step 4: Press on 'Save.'

How To Add Additional Keyboard Language

Launch into Settings > Languages & Input > Translation & Input

Select the language you want from the list of supported languages (Or use keyboard>keyboard>add language).

When your phone is connected to your PC via USB, you should see a notification asking if you want to use the keyboard input. Tap to accept and then select your language from the drop-down list.

Connecting Keyboard And Set Up

Step 1. Set up your devices and WiFi:

Always make sure to set your device as a secure WiFi network.

Make sure your device is connected to your phone via a good mobile WiFi network.

If you want to use it with a Bluetooth keyboard then make sure to set it up.

Step 2. Configure your Bluetooth keyboard and keyboard key position.

If you are using a Samsung keyboard then you have to follow this guide to configure the keyboard:

If you are using any other Bluetooth keyboard then you have to follow this guide to configure the keyboard:

For a Bluetooth device, check your Bluetooth device's information and make sure to set up the correct way to connect with the keyboard.

Step 3. Pairing the keyboard to the phone.

In this step, you have to pair your Bluetooth keyboard with your phone.

Type into your Bluetooth keyboard, select the 'searching for device' option, help you find your device, and then connect your phone.

Once you successfully connect your phone, the keyboard will show up on your phone.

Step 4. Entering words and typing the text.

In this step, you have to enter the text that you want to type on your keyboard.

Tap on the keys you want to enter and press them hard enough; when you press them, you will see a beep sound; after that, you can enter more text that you want to type. That's all you have to do, now you can start typing without any hassle.

How To Reset Your Device

STEP 1

Launch Settings Menu by swiping in from the left side of the screen.

STEP 2

Select Backup & Reset.

STEP 3

From the Backup & Reset menu, select 'Change Device settings.'

STEP 4

Select Reset Device settings.

STEP 5

Choose Reset Phone and click Confirm.

STEP 6

Enter your user password to confirm the changes.

CHAPTER ELEVEN

Locating And Setting Up Your Device Accessibility

You can find it under the Accessibility menu if you press on the Settings Gear icon, and further, on the list, you can find the following access keys:

Ease of Access: slider of phone from OFF to ON (The slider also controls the sound system's volume).

Swipe to control volume.

Speed control.

Keyboard control.

How to enable the Accessibility features

To enable it, go to Settings -> General -> Accessibility -> Swipe gestures.

You can also head over to the Accessibility option from the physical key 'L' to enable the other four options.

How to enable the 'Speed' key

If you want to control sound fast and quickly, then the Speed Key is the right option for you. You can find it under the Accessibility menu.

How to enable 'Keyboard Control

Keyboard Control is one of the favorite accessibility features of many users. By enabling it, you will be able to create multiple hand movements for the keyboard to be used. You can find it under the Accessibility menu.

How to disable Accessibility features on your device

Disabling it means you will not be able to access the key commands of the Accessibility options.

It can be disabled either from the Accessibility menu or from a physical key 'L' on your device

How to easily enable the Accessibility features on your device

Enabling Accessibility functions on your phone requires you to go to the Accessibility option from the physical key 'L' key.

To quickly enable all the key commands, press and hold the key 'L' until the word 'Skip' appears on the screen.

Getting Information About Your Device

To get more information about your device, go to the home screen, then click on settings; from there, click on "system." From the "system," click on "about phone," and you will see some information about your device.

Setting Up Your Emails

On your device, go to settings -> application manager -> settings -> apps -> then click the menu icon at the top of the screen. Select Google Apps, then again go to settings -> apps -> now, select Google and click OK.

Now, your settings should show the option to force stop Google search. 'Once this step is complete, you should get a message on your notification bar, 'Add Google Account. 'Select the option 'add Google account,' You should now see a new tab called, 'settings. 'Select the tab called 'network connection, 'and you will see the network connection type change to 'Sync & Online. '

The settings should show a new section, called 'automated setup, ' select the option to 'Set Up automatic setup. 'In this step, it will ask you some options, select the option that says 'Sign-in. 'The next step is to select the option that says, 'Sign in to Google account. 'After clicking on this option, you will see the following screen.

Now, enter the details that you want to enter here. Enter your Google username and password and click on 'Continue. '

After this, you should see the following screen.

It is also important to note that you should not forget this step, otherwise you will not be able to use Google, Samsung chat services. Once you do that, you will see the following screen.

Now in this section, you can select the option that says 'Sign in to Google account. 'Once you click on that, you should see the following screen.

Select the option that says 'I agree. 'Now, click on the check button. Select the option that says 'Confirm, 'and this will tell you the option to 'Finalize setup. '

Finally, you should see the following screen.

Now, you have successfully setup Google, Samsung chat services on your Samsung Galaxy S21 series but if you want to clear some space or disable the same, you can do that as well.

After you complete the steps mentioned above, you will get the following message, 'Google account is active. '

CHAPTER TWELVE

Understanding The Front And Back Camera Lenses

The Galaxy S21 Ultra has the most advanced camera setup we've seen from Samsung yet. It has four cameras, including two zoom lenses. The galaxy 21 Ultra is Samsung's premier flagship phone, and it brings a more advanced camera setup than any of the others.

There are four cameras on the back, a 108-megapixel known as your main camera, a 12-megapixel ultra-wide with autofocus and two zoom lenses, a 10-megapixel 10 times fold and Periscope zoom, and a traditional 10-megapixel three times telephoto, both with dual pixel autofocus.

Let's start with 12-megapixel photos from the main camera. There are plenty of results, detail, outstanding and dynamic range, almost no noise, and natural-looking colors.

Samsung's live focus mode is now called portrait mode. By default, the phone uses a two-time zoom crop from the main camera, so you can opt for a wide portrait to subject detection and separation are outstanding. The ultra-wide has autofocus, so you can use it to take close-up macro-style shots. They are sharp and colorful, with some very nice intricate details. Even though the S21 series' Ultra telephoto cameras have a 10-megapixel sensor, the output photos are 12-megapixels.

Three times zoom shots are decent with accurate colors, low noise, and great dynamic range. If you turn on night mode on the S21, the improvement is remarkable, there's a good detail and you get balanced sharpness, very low noise saturated colors, restored highlights, and well-developed shadows. Night mode photos from the main camera on the S21 are nearly identical to shooting an auto mode with the ultra-wide camera at night and will get you great results.

The night mode saves the day. It gets rid of the noise, improves the exposure restores clip highlights, and exposes more detail and shadow areas colors that look much better too. The results are very similar to all three smartphone models, except for small differences like the colors. When zooming in low light the S21 Ultra is the clear winner, thanks to the three times optical zoom and dedicated 10 times telephoto. The three times telephoto was able to take shots at night if it isn't too dark.

Similarly, that 10 times zoom camera will kick in only if there is sufficient light. The photos at night are good with surprisingly low noise and accurate colors, night mode isn't so useful with this camera though, it improves exposure otherwise, there isn't much improvement. If you're unable to make the phone stable, the outcome might result in blurriness.

The S21 Ultra has a 40-megapixel quad bare front-facing cam, which has autofocus is the same selfie cam you see on the S20 Ultra. By default, selfies come out in a crowd of five megapixels, but you can opt for a wider 10-megapixel photo. Overall, these are among the best we've seen from a smartphone. There's plenty of detail wide dynamic range, and spot-on colors. You can also shoot in the native 40-megapixels. And these are incredibly detailed great if that's what you're after in a selfie.

Moving on to video recording, the S21 Ultra can shoot selfie videos in 4k resolution, and a 30 FPS the quality is excellent. With enough resolution detail, great contrast and colors, a wide dynamic range, and low noise. We could say the same about the 4k footage at 30 FPS from the rear cameras as well. They're not the sharpest you've seen from a flagship, but they are excellent.

You also can shoot video from the main cam and 8k resolution at 24 FPS. It's quite soft and suffers from compression artifacts. It is useful as you can take snaps out of the 8k footage; this way you can capture a series of quick or exciting moments. Once you manually downsize the full resolution snaps, look decent, and electronic stabilization is available on all shooters in all modes, it does a great job smoothing out your footage. The Galaxy S21 Ultra delivers an excellent camera experience. It's the most versatile setup we've gotten yet from Samsung.

How To Quickly Launch The Camera

To launch the camera, go back to your home screen, from there, click on the camera icon on your screen, and it will instantly open up your camera app.

Taking Pictures With Your Camera

First, open up the camera app, then focus the lens of the camera on the object you will like to capture; once that is done, click on the middle icon on your camera screen to capture the image. It will automatically be saved in your gallery as soon as you click the shutter button. You can also use the lower button at the side of your device to capture the image.

Taking Videos

Open the camera app, then you will see a list of the option at the button of the screen, slide to where it says "video" then click on it, it will immediately change to video mode, to start recording; click on the middle round icon again until a red dot shows on it. Once the red dot appears, it will begin to record whatever is in front of the camera lens. Once you are done recording, click on the record button again, and it will save whatever you have recorded.

How To Use Single Take

Open the camera app, slide down below the shutter button for different options until you see "single take" click on it, and you can begin to take pictures.

AR Doodle Mode

You can use the AR feature to create beautiful and detailed drawings, and you can also use it to draw live sketches. You can use the AR doodle feature to create multi-colored and interesting drawings on your table or from the desktop on your cell phone. You need to keep your sketch pad in front of you and draw on a tabletop with realistic colors in your imagination. You can also draw and record your sketch on your mobile phone. Use your fingers and the new Samsung Galaxy S21 device to draw on the screen or monitor your mobile phone, tablet, or computer.

How to use AR doodle mode on your device

You can open the google sketchpad app on your device or your PC. Tap on the multi-colored pencil at the bottom of your screen to start drawing and watching a live sketch. The Google Sketchpad app has many drawing tools, and you can use several drawing tools at once on your mobile phone. You can draw in black and white on your Samsung device or use several color palettes to draw. The latest software on the Google Sketchpad has enabled the Samsung Galaxy S21 series to make live drawings and to bring your sketches with your colors of imagination. You can also use machine learning and artificial intelligence to create impressive drawings and to sketch on the Samsung Galaxy S21 series. Use the pen to draw a quick sketch of an object on the floor, on paper, or anywhere in your imagination. You can use the smart sensors of the device to easily draw on any surface of your phone.

Panorama Mode

STEP 1

You can also take a panorama on the device through Home Screen. To take the picture, all you have to do is click on Photo Menu and then tap on Panorama.

Step 2

Now, you will have to wait for a second until the picture gets taken.

Step 3

Now, double-click on the photo you took on your device's screen and then wait for a second.

Step 4

Tap on the back button on your phone or on the screen to resume to the Home Screen.

Step 5

That's it. The picture will appear on your screen.

Step 6

You can also use the picture gallery to browse the picture. Open the Gallery app and select the picture that you want to view.

Portrait Photo Mode

Open the camera app and select the Portrait photo mode option, and the phone automatically switches to the most suitable mode according to the subject.

Slow Motion

First, start by tapping on the camera button to open it. For now, you are in the standard photo mode. You change it by using the settings bar. Go to the right; there you have access to most of this camera; you have the slow-motion mode and the super-slow motion. You can pick whatever you need.

Click on the standard motion, and you can start recording the slow-motion video. When you are done, click on the big button at the center, and it will be saved to your gallery.

Hyperlapse

Open the camera app, then scroll to the right side and click on more; it will display various options in the camera, look for hyperlapse and click on it; you can use the big button at the center to record the video and also click on it to save the recorded video to your gallery.

How To Use Directors View

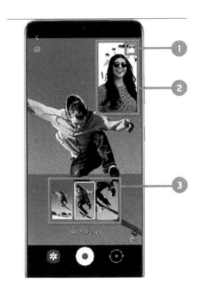

Directors view lets you record video with the front and rear cameras simultaneously

How to use it;

Go to the camera, tap on "more" then tap on "directors view."

Press the record button

Tap the thumbnail to switch between camera angles, wide, ultra-wide, telephoto. Capture the action and your reaction all at the same time with vlogger mode.

CHAPTER THIRTEEN

How To Launch And Set Up Bixby

Bixby can understand voice commands and can take selfies by holding your Galaxy S21 in your eyes. So far, the assistants are more focused on text and online commands, but it's only a matter of time before more functions are added. To perform them, Bixby relies on Samsung's voice control and uses visual cues (gestures and pictures) instead of keywords.

Step 1: Go to the Bixby voice settings. Click on the word 'Voice Access.' Next to the voice menu on the top right side of the screen. Click on the toggle switch to the 'On' position. Now, enter your voice code, which is sent to you from Samsung via SMS.

Step 2: Now, activate the Bixby voice by saying 'Hi Bixby.'

Turning Off Or Restarting Your Phone

To turn off your device, press and hold the power button, then click on "power off," and your device will go off.

Press and hold the power button for restarting your device. Once the Samsung logo is on the screen, it means your device is turned on and about to restart.

How To Change Your Screen Resolution

Go to Settings > About Phone > Screen resolution and then tap on the following options, choose 1080p, and choose default. The setting will be changed to 1080p. The resolution will be displayed on your screen. You'll be able to see the change on your Samsung Galaxy S21 series display.

Also, you can manually change the resolution of your screen by going to Settings > Display & Brightness and selecting Screen resolution and then select Full HD+ resolution.

Using Your Device Launcher And Customizing Widgets

First of all, you need to unlock this interface, go to the home screen, you can access it in several ways. The simplest way is by swiping to the left from the home screen or swiping to the right from the home screen to open. You can also open the home screen by swiping down from the top or swiping down from the top. Tap on the widgets of your choice. You can see there are two categories for widgets:

Regular Widget – those are standard widgets you can see every day on your home screen.

Selective Widget – these are widgets you can see a specific set of options like the alarm clock, messaging, reminders, and many others.

To customize these widgets, you need to go to the list of widgets you want to change, then long-press it. You will see that you have two buttons to choose from, either a dark or light theme for your widget.

For dark themes, hold on to the widget and then press the button. For light theme, press on the widget and then click on the option. Now, you can see a preview of the widget. If it's the light theme, then, you can see the app icon of the widget on the wallpaper. Tap on the screen to confirm the choice. You can now turn on or off the selected widget.

How To Add Application To Your Screen

The Samsung Galaxy S21 series features a touch screen that can be used for navigation, etc.; it also comes with a special feature that allows users to add applications to their home screen by touching the number of icons that are shown on their home screen. After this, you can use your finger on the screen to create a shortcut to the application. You need to select an application that you want to get on your home screen and drag the application from the phone's main screen to your home screen.

CHAPTER FOURTEEN

Customizing Your Dialer And Call Background

The dialer comes with an option for two different interfaces – phone and messaging. You can choose your preference by going to Phone app > Messaging app.

Go to Phone App > Messaging App and add a new message window.

Go to Phone App > Dialer and Add Number.

There's a call history link at the top right corner of the message window, so you can enter the details of a phone call you have received without having to switch between the Messaging and Phone apps.

To add a new dialer theme, you can choose from a selection of themes provided by Samsung or use the Google Now launcher. For a smoother transition, make sure you use the new Dialer theme to change the dialer. To do this, go to Phone app > Change icon.

Some of the default themes of the dialer are very colorful and bright but if you prefer to have a dialer that is more tranquil and calm, go to Settings > Color tab to adjust the color theme of the dialer.

You can enable the New Contacts option by pressing the menu button above the camera icon. Select Contacts then click on 'Add' in the search box at the top right.

Once added, check the 'Create group' option, and you'll be able to create contacts of up to 10 names.

Accessing Your Message Settings

You can control the message settings of the Samsung Galaxy S21 series in both external and internal settings. In the external setting, tap on the three dots at the top-right corner of the screen. You can choose Message Settings in the following steps.

Enable messaging settings:

Tap on the message settings in the upper right corner. Then select enable messages setting.

In the internal setting, you can select message settings in the following steps.

Go to Settings > Messaging & instant messaging, then select the message settings.

Important Note:

If you are not able to access message settings on the Samsung Galaxy S21 series, then delete old messages as it is not working properly.

CHAPTER FIFTEEN

Updating Your Device OS

As soon as the update is available on your device, go to Settings>About phone>Check for updates. Wait until the update is available, and then tap on 'Install now.' The updates can take a while to complete, so if you don't receive the OTA, you can manually check for the update by going to settings> applications> Software update> Check for updates.

Make sure your device is charged at least 50 percent battery to speed up the installation process. After the OTA update, the device will get new features like picture-in-picture, notification dots, adaptive theme support, Autofill framework, faster booting, enhanced security update, notification dots, and more.

Charging Your Device

1. Plug the charger into the wall or an AC power socket

2. Turn on your device into "Use Mobile Data" mode. Press the Volume UP key on the device, and the Device switch icon on the Home screen

3. Now, turn on "Backlight Mode" and press "Start" to switch back to normal mode.

4. It may take up to 1–2 hours for Samsung Galaxy S21 devices to be fully charged.

CONCLUSION

The Samsung Galaxy S21 has a new web feature and an ultra-wideband; this wireless communication technology makes it possible to use Samsung SmartThings to locate galaxy devices, even when offline or communicate with your vehicle to perform certain tasks in the future.

For added productivity, the top-of-the-line variant also features WiFi 6 which is said to be four times faster than normal WiFi. It is powered by a five-nanometer processor and promises a 20% increase in CPU performance, 35% increase in GPU performance and an AI that's twice as efficient and faster than previous versions,

At the beginning of this book, we told you some of the things to expect from this book like how to update your device to the latest version, how to get the most from your Galaxy S21 camera features, how to make use of E-sims on this device and add additional keyboard languages to your device. We hope this book has made you understand the Samsung Galaxy S21 series a lot better. Users and intended buyers of this device should note that this device does not have a slot for an external memory card/ micro SD card, which means you cannot use external storage on the Samsung Galaxy S21 series.

Samsung Galaxy S21 Camera Guide

The Complete User Manual for Beginners and Pro to Master Professional Cinematic Videography and Photography Tips and Tricks Using Samsung Galaxy S21, S21 Plus & Ultra

INTRODUCTION

The Samsung S21 has a front facing camera just like the other models; the front camera is located at the middle top area of the Samsung S21 device, just right below the speaker. A little space to the left is where the proximity sensor is located, although it cannot be seen physically. The image below shows the complete description of what we're trying to explain above. You can also see the volume increase and decrease keys at the side of the device which can be used to take photos instead of tapping the shutter button. Also, the volume keys can also be used to take screenshots or perform a screen record when held together with the power button. The front facing camera is mainly used for taking selfies and video calling purposes.

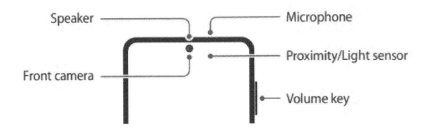

Speaker — Microphone

Proximity/Light sensor

Front camera —

Volume key

Now let talk about the rear cameras, the Samsung S21 model has three rear cameras accompanied with a single flash light. The rear cameras are arranged horizontally on top of each other with a barrier making it look specific. The flash light is located just outside the barrier and right beneath it is a microphone. The rear cameras are of three different types of cameras called; the ultra-lens, Ultra-wide lens and the telephoto lens, each having a different megapixel. Capturing crisp and HD photos, you'd need to make use of the rear cameras, also for capturing wide areas such as valleys, mountains or skyscrapers, the ultra-wide camera will do the job perfectly.

This guide contains everything you need to know about the Samsung S21 cameras, start your journey as a professional photographer as you read this amazing guide.

CHAPTER ONE

How to quickly open the Camera app

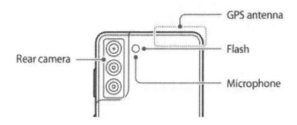

How do you get to the camera application on your Samsung S21 device? It's pretty easy and normally you should be able to do it. The camera application is one of the mostly used pre-installed application on any device, although this is depending on the user, but, seven out of ten people uses the camera application often more than other apps, which is why the camera app is usually located in the lock screen for easy access.

There are several ways to quickly open the camera application, the first of which is from the lock screen. In the lock screen, there are usually three options below, and they're the *call option, unlock option and the camera option.* Users should note that the call option is only meant for emergency calls and you'll be able to make normal calls if the device is unlocked.

Once in the lock screen, you can swipe upwards from the camera option icon and it'll take you to the camera app immediately, with this you'd be able to take pictures and view them while your screen is still locked, although some of other camera features might be restricted in use till you unlock your device.

Another quick way to open the camera application is by unlocking your device and navigating to the camera application from the home screen, and tap on it. This way, you'll get all features of the camera application and you'd be able to view all previous and present pictures.

How to take a picture

In this section, our primary aim is to teach you how to take pictures with the camera application, all you need to do is follow the procedures given below;

1.   Navigate to the camera app and open it using any of the methods we've explained in the first section. *(NB: Users should note that the camera app can also be launched by double clicking the side key, also when launching the camera from the lock screen, be aware that some features might not be available to you.)*

2.   Focus the camera on a particular image; tap the center of the image so the camera would focus on it.

3.   After focusing the camera and you're satisfied with what you're seeing, simply tap the shutter button

below to take the shot. The white circular button beneath the camera interface is the shutter button.

(See image below)

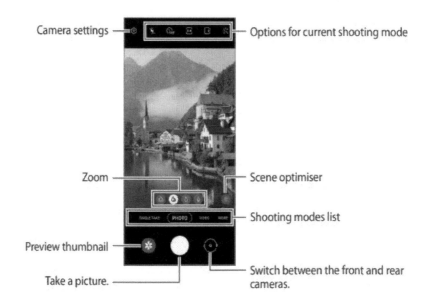

Camera settings — Options for current shooting mode

Zoom — Scene optimiser

Shooting modes list

Preview thumbnail —

Take a picture. — Switch between the front and rear cameras.

4.   Choose the shooting mode you prefer from the section above, also you zoom in, switch cameras and explore the camera settings. The image above shows it all for better understanding.

5.   The preview thumbnail can be used to view pictures that have been taken; however this varies

depending on the shooting mode and camera being used.

6. It is advisable to take images from a good distance in order not to zoom in or out because zoomed pictures might not give you the quality you require.

7. If you take a picture and it's blurry, use a clean cloth or tissue to dab the camera lens, then take the shot again.

8. If any of the lenses are damaged, the camera may not work for some features.

9. That's just a simple way to take a picture using the Samsung galaxy S21.

How to record a video

Recording a simple video on Samsung S21 is similar to taking a picture, users can record video easily just by tapping the video record shutter button. You can also switch between different video modes, choosing your preferred mode.

In this section, we would be teaching you how to take a simple video record using your new Samsung S21.

1.   Once in the camera app, swipe the shooting modes list to move to VIDEO or choose VIDEO from the list.

2.   Select the video recording shutter button to start recording a video.

3.   While recording a video, you might want to change in between the front and back cameras, swipe upwards or downwards to switch to either front or rear camera. Also, you can tap the option to perform the switch function.

4.   Tap the shutter button again to stop recording the video.

5.   Zooming a video for a long period while recording might result in low-quality results. This is done not to cause overheating for your device. So it is advisable to reduce zooming while recording a video.

That's how to perform a simple video recording using your Samsung S21, in the coming chapters of this book; we'll talk more about videos.

CHAPTER TWO

Rear Camera capabilities

The rear camera ability of the Samsung S21 is the real deal of the device; it is one big reason why most users go for the Samsung S21. The incredible features and ability that the Samsung S21 camera possesses will be discussed extensively in this section.

First of all, the rear cameras of the Samsung S21 possess four (*Actually Three Main types*) different types of lenses with each performing different functions in a photograph. There's the Ultra wide lens, Wide lens, Telephoto lens 1, and Telephoto lens 2. Samsung S21+ and Ultra doesn't possess the Telephoto 2 lens camera at the rear, it is only available in the Samsung S21.

For specifications, the Samsung S21 ultra wide lens is 12Megapixels, F2.2, 120° spanning up to 13mm. The wide lens possesses 108Megaixels, F1.8, 83° spanning 24mm while the first telephoto lens possesses 10Megapixels, F2.4, 35° and spans up to 72mm. The last but not the least of which is the Telephoto 2 possesses the same 10Megapixels, F4.9, 10° and will span almost 240mm.

These specifications are what the Samsung S21 rear cameras are made of, which is why they're mostly needed by individuals for photography reasons.

Front Camera capabilities

In this section we should be looking at the front camera capabilities of the Samsung S21, individuals like taking crisp and clear HD selfies, which is why the Samsung S21 front selfie camera is just the best answer.

For specifications the front camera of the Samsung S21 possesses 40Megapixels which captures very beautiful and detailed selfies. In the coming chapters of this book, we'll talk more about the front camera and what it can do.

What is the Aperture mode?

As a photography lover, there are some terms that shouldn't be new to you, one of them is the Aperture

Mode. In this section, we would be talking about the aperture mode, what it works for.

Firstly, what is Aperture? It can simply be defined as a narrow space in a lens in which light passes through into the camera. The aperture is expressed in numbers such as f2.2 f1.8 as we've shown in the rear camera specifications above. Adjusting the aperture means that you're increasing or decreasing the space in which light comes right into the lens of the camera, typically this is done by the camera lens. That's everything about the Aperture mode.

CHAPTER THREE

How to take burst photos

This section teaches you how to take burst photos easily on your Samsung galaxy S21, it's quite easy. If you don't know what burst photos are, here's the explanation below;

Burst photos are series of the different photos taken almost at once, trying it out would give you a practical example of what burst mode really is. Burst photos is mostly used when capturing moving items, it gives you the opportunity to choose from many similar photos. Now that you've gotten the idea of what burst mode is, now go below and practice it using your new Samsung galaxy S21.

1.   Open the camera application from the home screen of your Samsung S21.

2.   On the top right corner of the camera interface, you'll see something like a setting icon, click on it and it'll open up a list of options.

3.   Select the option which says *swipe shutter button to* and then choose **take burst photos.**

4.   Now go back to your camera interface and swipe the shutter button downwards, immediately your device will start taking a series of shots, the counts will be displayed on the shutter button so you know when to stop.

5.   Now you can go to your gallery and choose a photo of your choice from the series you've taken.

6.   That's how to take a burst photo.

How to use optimal image stabilization

Optical image Stabilization or OIS is a feature available on both the Samsung galaxy S20 and S21 device. This feature makes both software and hardware processes that typically allow you to take very clear and detailed photos in any environment even if there isn't enough light. Because of the multi Camera rear camera that the Samsung galaxy S21 possesses, the camera system has dual OIS which is used for steady capturing and this doesn't matter if you're using the wide or telephoto lenses.

The OIS makes you take photos anytime of the day and still get the correct clear and detailed image you need.

If you wish to activate the video stabilization of your Samsung S21 device, try using the procedures below;

1.   Launch the camera application from the home screen of your Samsung Galaxy S21.

2.   Click on the settings icon at the top right corner of the device

3.   Swipe downwards and activate video stabilization, if you activated it already and want to deactivate it, toggle the switch.

4.   After this, go back to the camera interface and continue your video session.

5.   Doing this will allow the video to be more stable than usual.

How to choose the best external device for your Galaxy S21

Samsung S21 no longer makes use of Micro SD as they ditched the idea in 2020, so if you'd be thinking that the Samsung S21 may possess Micro SD slot, you're totally wrong. There's no Micro SD slot, and that's why we've decided to write this section in this guide is to show you some of the best alternative external devices you can use for your Samsung S21 device.

Here are some nice external devices we've listed below:

1.   **Samsung T7 500GB portable SD:** This is the first and most popular external device that can be recommended for your new Samsung

S21 device. It is covered in an incredible design that can stand many dangerous effects. The external device comes with USB-C cables right inside the box upon purchase. Because of the durable design and very fast transfers from your Samsung S21, that is why we recommend it as the first and best alternative external devices. The Samsung T7 500GB portable SD can be gotten for $90 only on Amazon, price may vary on other online stores.

2.   **Anker SD card reader:** if you possess a Micro SD card previously and you and some

important data inside the SD card, then you'd need an external card reader to access those files. The Anker SD card reader is one of the top picks card readers for the job. Durable and portable, the Anker SD card reader possesses slots for both Micro SD and normal SD cards. The Anker SD card reader can be gotten for $13 only on Amazon; price may vary on other online stores.

3.   Samsung Duo Plus 256 GB USB-C USB 3.1 flash drive: This amazing flash drive gives you the ease of access to the files saved on your drive. With this device, you'll be able to transfer photos and videos right from your device into the flash drive using a USB-C cable. It's a good backup for your photos and videos, the Samsung Duo plus cost only $45 on Amazon, value on other online stores may vary.

These three external devices are the most valued and popular external device, which you could use to back up your Samsung galaxy S21. Individuals are advised to choose according to their financial abilities.

CHAPTER FOUR

How to use portrait mode

The portrait mode is an incredible feature which is available in new versions of android devices, this feature is also available in the Samsung galaxy S21 and it's more efficient and amazing. In this section, we would be teaching you everything you need to know about portrait mode and how you can make use of it, thereby improving your photography skills.

The portrait mode is a simple image that blurs the background of a subject when captured, giving the main subject a sharp and highly detailed look. The background blurriness gives the photo a kind of soft feeling and makes it look cooler than normal snapshots.

Now that you know what portrait mode is, the steps below will teach you how to take images using the portrait mode;

1.   Open the camera application from the home screen of your Samsung galaxy S21

2.   On the camera interface, swipe till you find MORE

3.   Select Portrait from the option

4.   Choose any of the portrait effects that's available.

5.   Also select a background effect that you'd like

6.   Background intensity can also be adjusted to your preferred way, this means you might not want the background entirely blur or too blurry,

7.   After all adjustments, select the shutter button to take the photo, hold still till your photo appears in the thumbnail.

8.   That's it, you just took a shot using portrait mode!

How to use night mode

Night mode is another popular feature that is also available in many other devices as well as the Samsung galaxy S21. The feature is one of a kind, because it allows you to take clear and crisp pictures in an environment with low light.

To capture a photo using the night mode feature, we've shown steps below;

1.   Open the camera application from the home screen of your Samsung galaxy S21

2.   On the camera interface, swipe till you find MORE

3.   Select Night mode from the option, the icon is a crescent moon.

4.   Focus the camera on the subject you wish to capture.

5.   Afterwards, hold down the shutter button, and you'll see that the crescent moon will start turning into a full moon.

6.   Once it turns into a complete full moon, your shot has been taken, and you'll see the brightness in a low light environment.

7.   That's it, simple right? You just took a shot using night mode.

About scene Optimizer

This is another common term that you need to know as a photographer, the scene optimizer, although first introduced in the old Samsung S9 device is now available across many Samsung devices which include the Samsung galaxy S21. Scene optimizer is a feature that is placed in the Samsung Ai camera which helps it to detect subjects automatically without you having to focus on it; also it adjusts beautifully, helping you take cool images. The scene optimizer modifies the exposure, white balance and contrast of an environment, it also chooses modes.

Some of the modes it chooses includes; vehicles, drinks, Face, baby, person, dog, cat, food, sunrise, city, snow, rain, waterfall, sky, text, greenery, mountain, sunset, and many others.

To use the scene optimizer on your Samsung galaxy S21, please use the following procedures below;

1.   Open the camera application from the home screen of your Samsung galaxy S21

2.   Scene optimizer is available on the camera app by default, so there's no worry about activation.

3.   Hold till the camera detects a subject, and then tap the shutter button to take the shot.

4.   That's it; you just took a photo that was scene optimized.

CHAPTER FIVE

How to activate focus enhancer

If you wish to get a better focus when capturing photos using your Samsung galaxy S21, then you should activate the focus enhancer feature. This feature allows you to get better focus on subjects and objects while capturing, thereby producing detailed and well captured images.

To enable the focus enhancer, follow the steps shown below;

1.   Open the camera application from the home screen of your Samsung galaxy S21

2.   Select Photo Mode

3.   Tap the screen to reveal hidden options on the panels

147

4.   There's a white double circled icon on the bottom left of your device

5.   Select that icon to activate focus enhancer, see image below for better explanation.

6.   After focusing, select the shutter button to capture an image and hold still till it's shown in the thumbnail.

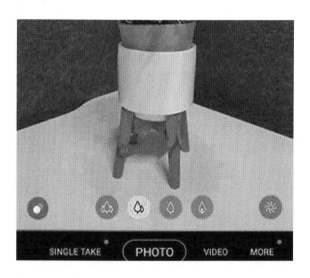

7.   That's it; you just captured a photo after using the focus enhancer!

Zooming

The rear camera lenses contribute to the zooming ability of the Samsung galaxy S21, as we discussed earlier, there are approximately four lenses on the rear of the Samsung S21 device, there's the standard zoom, followed by an ultra-wide lens, 3x optical zoom and 10x optical zoom respectively. With all these lenses, you can perform a 30x zoom on your Samsung galaxy S21; the next section will be teaching you how to use the space zoom feature.

How to use space zoom

Space zooming is just another name for the 30x zoom, with the Samsung S21, you can zoom a picture up to 30x and we'll be showing you that in this section.

To space zoom on your new Samsung galaxy S21, follow the procedures that we outlined below;

1.   Open the camera application from the home screen of your Samsung galaxy S21

2.	On the screen tap the zoom feature, it's a number on the screen, or just pinch the screen and spread your hands.

3.	You'll see ratio of your zoom below as you zoom, see the picture below;

4.	Drag the slider till you hit the 30x zoom.

5.	The image below shows 3x zoom

6.   The image below shows 10x zoom

7.   The image below shows 30x zoom

How to use live focus

The live focus is only available in video mode in the Samsung S21, on the note20; you'd see a live focus for images. In this section, we'll be teaching you everything about live focus and how you can use it.

The live focus video is almost the same with the portrait video, because they make use of the same options, using the live focus mode, it adds an effect to any video you're recording. Now to use the live focus feature, follow the steps we've outlined below;

1.   Open the camera application from the home screen of your Samsung galaxy S21

2.   Once on the camera interface, swipe to the right till you find MORE, select it and a panel of list will drop down.

3.   Choose Live Focus Video.

4.   There's a circle in the bottom right corner of the viewfinder, tapping the circle reveals four options which are; Blur, Glitch, Color point and Big circle.

5.   Choose any one you like and tap the shutter button to begin recording. See image below.

How to use super slow-mo

As a photography freak, you'd know how to record a video using slow-mo; however, there's a better option, which is the super slow-mo. In this section, we would be showing you how to perform a super slow-mo recording.

To record videos using the super slow-mo feature, use the steps below;

1.   Open the camera application from the home screen of your Samsung galaxy S21

2.	Once on the camera interface, swipe to the right till you find MORE, select it and a panel of list will drop down

3.	Choose super slow-mo

4.	Select either Automatic or Manual

5.	Automatic mode records as soon as movements is detected within the square

6.	Manual mode will record as soon as you press the shutter button

7.	If you chose automatic, focus the camera on the subject and await a movement

8.	If you choose manual, once the camera is focused, and the subject has begun its movement, select the shutter button.

9.	Tap the shutter button again to stop the record.

10. That's the simple way of recording a super slow-mo video on Samsung S21.

CHAPTER SIX

How to add effects while on video call

During a video call, Samsung users can use different effects, which the other caller can see regardless of whatever phone they're using. However, this depends on the application and also depends on the device too. If you wish to use the video call effects while performing a video call, you'll need to activate the feature first. In this section, we would be showing you how to use effects during a video call.

To use video calling effects, follow the steps that we've carefully outlined below;

1.   Launch the settings application on your Samsung galaxy S21 home screen

2.   Swipe downwards till you see ADVANCED FEATURES

157

3.   Select it.

4.   Go down the list of options till you get to the bottom

5.   Select VIDEO CALL EFFECTS

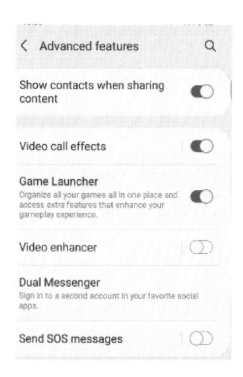

6.   If the effects toggle is deactivated, activate by toggling the switch again

7.   Choose the Background effect you wish to use.

After performing every step we listed above, you can now use video calling effects when you're performing a video call. Although it depends on the application, as for now, the video call effects works for Google Duo, Cisco WebEx, Zoom and Microsoft Teams.

Now, if you have any of the apps listed above, you can try out making video calls with it, you'll see an icon at the top corner of the device, select it and you'd be able to choose the effect you want.

Also, it is important to note that the video calling feature was first introduced in the Samsung S21 series and is not available in previous Samsung devices.

How to activate show palm

For a photographer lover, you might have heard about Show palm; however, if you haven't heard about Show palm, we'll be showing you everything about Show palm in this section.

Firstly, what's Show Palm? Show palm is an easy way to take selfies without having to tap the shutter button allowing you to make a perfect posture and taking shots without having to stress pressing the shutter button. The Show palm is mostly used for selfies, although it may seem embarrassing to do in public.

Now that you know what Show palm is, let's show you how to activate the Show palm and also how to make use of it.

To activate Show palm, follow the instructions we've outlined below;

1.   Launch the camera application from your Samsung galaxy S21 home screen

2.   Select the settings icon at the top right corner of the camera interface.

3.   Go down the list till you find the **Front camera** settings

4.   Toggle the switch next to the Show palm option

Doing the above activates Show palm, now the below steps will guide you on how to use Show palm.

1.   Launch the camera application from your Samsung galaxy S21 home screen

2.   Tap the switch button to change over to the front selfie camera

3.   Place the camera in front of you, if there are friends behind you, let them appear to.

4.   Now showcase the palm of your hand in front of the selfie camera *(NB: Your other hand)*

5.   A yellow square like stuff will suddenly appear on your hand, when this happens, it means that the camera has detected your palm.

6.   A two seconds timer would be quickly initiated and a selfie would be taken.

7.   The rule is, make sure you remove your hand from the front camera once the timer is activated.

Activating 8K video

Recording videos in 8k is the best because it'd bring out the quality and HD crisp video that you require. Maybe you bought your Samsung S21 for filming or video recording purposes, the 8K video would be a very unique feature to you. In this section, we'll be showing you how to activate and record videos using 8K.

In other to activate and start recording your videos in 8K, follow the steps that we've carefully outlined below;

1.   Launch the camera application from the Samsung galaxy S21 home screen

2.   Select VIDEO to switch to video mode in the camera interface.

3.   You'll see an icon located at the top right corner of the video mode interface, it's the resolution icon, select it and set the resolution to 8k which is 24 frames per second.

4.   When your subject is ready to be filmed, select the shutter button to begin the record.

5.   Tap the shutter button again to end the video when you're done. Videos recorded will be saved in your gallery.

However, users should note that 8K videos use up a lot of space on the Samsung device, and the S21 series being a device that doesn't make use of Micro SD card; you might not enjoy it very well unless you get a perfect external storage device.

In the next chapter, we would show you how to add background music to your videos and some other features.

CHAPTER SEVEN

How to apply background music to video clip

Did you record a great film while using the incredible 8K feature? And you wish to add music to it? Then this section is for you, in this section we would be teaching you how to add background music to your videos.

The great thing about adding background music to your videos is that, on Samsung galaxy S21, you don't need to download any application as the inbuilt Samsung video editor is perfect for the job.

To add background music to your video, use the steps we've outlined below;

1.   Launch the gallery application from your Samsung S21 home screen

2.	Select the video that you wish to add background music to

3.	Choose EDIT YOURSELF

4.	Select the pencil icon, which is located in the left corner beneath the screen, after you choose that, you'll be taken to the Samsung video editor.

5.	Now you'll be able to add background music and do a lot of other stuff on your Samsung video editor, it's very easy.

How to join multiple video clips to make a video

Combining or joining multiple video clips to make a video can be easily done using almost the same process as the one above, this is because you're going to be using the same internal Samsung video editor. In this section, we would show you briefly how to join or combine multiple video clips to make one whole video.

The below steps will guide you through in combining videos and making a whole video out of it:

1.   Open the gallery application from the home screen of your Samsung galaxy S21

2.   Choose one of the videos which is part of the clip you want to combine

3.   Choose the edit icon at the bottom left corner of the screen, looking like a pencil.

4.   Choose Add, it is located at the top of the video editor interface

5.   Select all the videos you want to combine with the first one

6.   Images can also be picked too.

7.   Select done when you've finished choosing

8.   The video timeline will display at the bottom of the screen.

9.   Select save, located at the top of the video editor interface to complete your combined video.

CHAPTER EIGHT

Backup

Backup simply means backing up your device, this is a very good thing to do as no one can predict the future, which means no one will know the absolute time that their device would get spoiled or damaged which can lead to loss of data and files if not properly backed up.

Backing up files can be done in several ways which include backing up with external devices, backing up with one drive and backing up with Google cloud storage, anyone you wish to back up with is perfect, but in this guide, we're only allowed to give you procedures on how to backup with One Drive.

However, we can give you a brief explanation on backing up with external devices, to back up your Samsung S21 with your external device; you need to continue sending any files and data into the external devices either on a weekly basis or daily basis. So all files on your Samsung S21 will be duplicated in the external device.

How to backup videos and photos to onedrive account

This section is a very straightforward one; we'll be showing you how you can back up your device using the inbuilt OneDrive cloud storage, the OneDrive cloud storage gives you 30GB of free storage space for you to store your important files and data. Some of the things you can backup includes videos, documents, music and pictures. After backing up, you can easily access backed up files from a PC anywhere in the world, all you'd need to do is visit onedrive.live.com. Also, updating your settings to automatic backup can keep you safe from losing files as your device would be backed up automatically any time it is connected to the internet.

Here's how to back up files with OneDrive below;

1.   Slide up to reveal the app menu screen on your Samsung galaxy S21.

2.   Go to Microsoft Apps folder, and choose OneDrive.

3.   If you have a OneDrive account before, just select Sign in and fill in your email and password, but if you do not possess a OneDrive account, simply tap Sign up to create one instantly.

4.   Select the upload option, and then choose any document or files you wish to back up.

5.   You should be aware that backing up your device will cost you a lot of data subscriptions.

Also, you can sync your gallery with OneDrive to help you backup your photos easily, syncing your gallery with OneDrive, you'd be able to access the photos from any other device. Here's how to sync your gallery with OneDrive;

1.   Launch the gallery app from your Samsung galaxy S21 app menu

2.   Choose Menu, it's the three horizontal lines at the bottom.

3.   Select settings; now activate the option next to **sync with OneDrive.**

4.   Now your entire gallery has been synced with OneDrive, you can easily access them on the OneDrive Website.

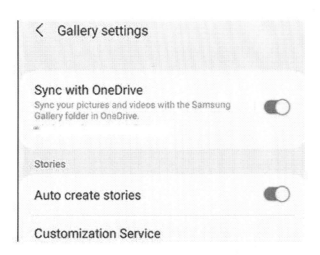

How to resize your image

You might want to use specific images for some reasons and you need to resize them to fit in to the requirements, don't worry! Resizing images just got easier with your Samsung galaxy S21. In this section, we would be showing the simple steps on how to resize your image.

To resize your image follow the detailed steps below;

1.   Launch the gallery application from your Samsung galaxy S21 app screen

2.   Choose any image you wish to resize.

3.   Select the pencil icon which stands for editing

4.   You'll see three dots on the top right corner of the editing interface, select it.

5.   Choose **resize** on the list that comes up.

6.   Modify to your preferred resized percentage then select done to authenticate changes.

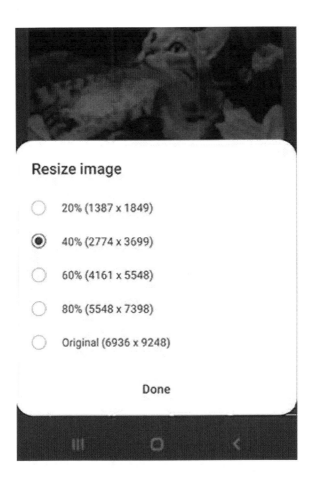

7.   After resizing your photo, you'll see in the image details that the size was reduced to your preferred percentage.

That's all; if you performed the steps above, you've successfully resize an image, now you can try it on other images that you wish to resize.

CHAPTER NINE

How to convert HEIF photo to JPEG

HEIC photo format cannot be viewed or used on Androids unless you convert them to JPEG, although, Apple has now allowed their devices to support HIEC photo format but Androids which Samsung is included haven't thought about the idea yet, which means you still have to convert your HEIC photo format to JPEG if you want to make use of it on the Samsung galaxy S21.

In this section, we would be showing you how to convert the HIEC photo format to JPEG, it's simple and easy, all you have to do is follow the procedures carefully.

Samsung doesn't have any image conversion tool or application that can convert HIEC photos to JPEG, so we'll be showing you some third party apps that can help you convert HIEC photo formats to JPEG. We'll be showing you one application and one website, so you can pick anyone you require.

Because there are many third party apps that can convert HIEC to JPEG we have chosen the best and most popular app for you, which is called LUMA. If you have a HIEC photo format and you want to convert to JPEG, you should download LUMA on your Samsung galaxy S21. Follow the procedures below to complete the conversion.

1.   Launch playstore from the home screen of your Samsung Galaxy S21.

2.   Search for LUMA and complete the download, afterwards install the LUMA app.

3.   The LUMA app is free from ads and is storage friendly.

4.   Launch the LUMA app and wait for it to load

5.   You'll see a screen with different options below, choose FROM HIEC since you're converting HIEC images to JPEG

6.   Select the addition + like icon, once you do that, two options will be presented to you, which are *Open single image and Open images folder.*

7.   The Open single image option allows you to select images one by one for the conversion why the Open images folder allows you to open any folder that possesses multiple HIEC images.

8.   Selecting Open single image, you can simply choose the image you want to convert individually, after choosing, simple select SAVE AS JPEG

9.   In the blink of an eye LUMA converts the image to JPEG, it's important to note that specifying where the images are saved are necessary, so you'd know where your new JPEG files are located.

10. If you have a folder filled with HIEC images and you want to convert all, simply select the Open image folder, and choose the folder, select images you wish to convert, then select CONVERT.

Now that you know how to use the LUMA app to convert HIEC images to JPEG, it's normal for us to give you another alternative in case you don't like using apps.

HIECTOJPEG is the best website you can use if you don't prefer using applications, the website is straightforward, we don't need to explain the procedures in steps for you to get it. Just visit HIECtoJPEG and upload your HIEC image and process them, download them once you're done. Easy as pie.

How to customize selfie color tone

After taking selfies, you may not like the color tone that's displaying, don't worry it's changeable. Changing the selfie color tone helps you modify images to your taste and preference. For those that prefer warm color tones on their selfies, Samsung has a feature for you. In this section, we would be teaching you how to customize and modify your selfie tone.

This hidden Samsung trick allows you to choose from different color tones saving you the stress of going through photo editing apps searching for filters and effects so you can change the color balance and temperature. Samsung color tones give you the warm and natural look that your image deserves. Changing the color tone doesn't take much of a step.

Here's how to perform the function below:

1.   Launch the camera application from your Samsung galaxy S21 home screen

2.   Switch your camera to selfie mode

3.   Select the setting icon which is located at the top left corner of the camera interface

4.   Go downwards till you see the Selfie color tone option

5.   Choose it, and then select your preferred color tone.

How to activate tracking autofocus

First of all, what is Autofocus? Auto focus is a feature that allows you to focus or lock a subject when taking snapshots, when it is locked; you get sharper and clearer images. The autofocus tracking works for situations whereby the object or subject is moving such as during sports, children and pets. In this section, we would be showing you how to activate the tracking Autofocus.

Use the steps available below to activate the feature above:

1.   Launch the camera app on your Samsung galaxy S21 home screen

2.   Go to photo mode

3.   Select any area on the screen, and then choose the lock icon to enable Autofocus. After activation, you'll be able to adjust and modify the light exposure around the shot by sliding and moving the bar until you get your preferred taste.

4.   After modification and focusing, select the shutter button to capture the shot.

5.   When the photo is captured, it'll appear in the thumbnail, tap it to view.

6.   That's for autofocus, now to activate tracking autofocus so you can capture moving objects easily, select the settings icon which is located at the top left corner of the camera's interface.

7.   Go downwards till you see tracking Autofocus, activate it.

8.   Now go back to the camera app and try capturing your unstable Toddler, moving objects or pets, they'll be kept in focus no matter how unstable they are.

CHAPTER TEN

How to activate voice command

Samsung has come up with another incredible feature which is available in the camera application, as a photography lover, this feature is one of the best for you. The Samsung galaxy S21 was specifically built to suit the needs of photography and videography that individuals want. Which is why in this guide, we would be showing every feature that concerns the camera app.

Because of the incredible and mouth watering features that Samsung has added to their camera application, even beginner photographers can take pictures that look like what should have been taken by a professional.

The voice command feature of the camera application is actually available in other devices, but if you're not familiar with android devices then you might get stuck in trying to activate it. That's why we've added it to this guide. In this section, we would be showing you how you can activate the voice command.

Following the procedures below, you'll find out how to take selfies just by using voice commands;

1.   Launch the camera application from your Samsung galaxy S21 home screen.

2.   Select the settings icon, which is located at the top left corner of the camera screen.

3.   Once in the settings screen, go downwards till you see **shooting modes**

4.   In the next screen, you'll see a list of shooting modes displayed for you, some of which are; show palm, floating shutter button, press volume keys and voice commands.

5.   Toggle the voice command switch to enable the voice command feature.

6.   After activating the feature, go back to your camera interface and use the voice commands to take pictures, you can use; "shoot", "cheese", "smile" and "capture" if you also wish to record a video using voice command just say "record video".

7.   This makes taking selfies and rear photo images with your friends easier and more fun.

In previous chapters of this book, we've shown you how to use the show palm feature too, that's another feature you can try out with your friends. To deactivate the voice command feature, use the same steps above and toggle the voice command switch again. However, we think most photography lovers will love using the command feature as it is stress free and would help you take pictures without the need of a tripod.

How to save photos and videos in high efficient

In this era smartphones does not only satisfy your multitasking needs such as watching videos, browsing the internet and maybe reading an eBook at the same time, there are hundreds of things that your smartphone can now perform, all what we've been talking about in this guide, I'm sure you never knew your device can actually do it, except for a few common ones. In this guide, we'll be showing you how you can save up photos and videos in high efficiency.

Saving images and videos in HEIF format is pretty easy, you just have to set it up in settings, the procedures below will take you through;

1.   Launch the settings application from your Samsung galaxy S21 home screen

2.   Choose **Format and Advanced options**

3.   Activate the switch of HEIF pictures

4.   Go over to Video mode and choose **Advanced recording**

5.   Enable the High efficiency video switch

6.   That's all, very simple and straightforward.

Doing this, Samsung galaxy S21 will now save video and photos in HEIF formats and won't compromise any detail or quality when saving. HIEF formats are smaller than the regular JPEG formats.

You can also convert the HEIF formats back to JPEG if need be, just head to Google and look for the best site that converts HEIF images to JPEG.

Activating HDR+10 shooting

HDR+ 10 which full meaning is High Dynamic range + 10 is a feature that gives your photos and videos standard reproduction of color. It is a feature built specifically to enhance color range as well as dynamic brightness. In this section, we'll be showing you how to use the HDR+ 10 feature to shoot videos with a wide range of colors and depth, bringing out your videos and photos more vivid and true to life.

It is therefore important to note that the HDR+10 feature is not available when video is being recorded at 60 frames per second. The HDR+10 feature will not work unless you activate it in the camera settings, some Samsung devices do not possess the HDR+10 feature, so that's an addition to you for getting the Samsung galaxy S21.

Below are the steps you should follow to activate the HDR+10 feature;

1.   Launch the camera application from the home screen of your Samsung galaxy, S21.

2.   Select the settings icon; it's located at the top left corner of the camera interface.

3.   Select REAR VIDEO SIZE, and then tap 16:9, also set the resolution to FHD 1920 X 1080. It is important to note that HDR+10 will only work with that video resolution.

4.   Go back, and then select **Advanced recording options** in the camera settings.

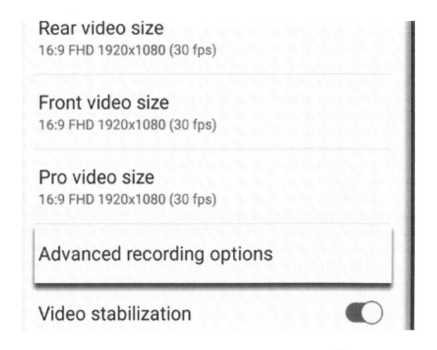

5.   Select the HDR+10 switch.

6.   That's all; you can now take your videos in HDR+10.

CHAPTER ELEVEN

Extracting high-resolution image from a video

After taking a video in 8k, you can still take a screenshot image from that video, this is known as extracting a high-resolution image from a video and that's what we would be teaching you in this section.

Extracting high-resolution images from a video is pretty easy and doesn't take a whole lot of process.

Here's how to do it below;

1.   Launch the gallery application from the app screen of your Samsung S21

2.   Select or pick any 8K video that you've recorded.

3.   Choose or tap the capture button, it's located at the top left corner of the screen.

4.   This takes the shot, you can also take more shots from the video footage, as much as you like.

5.   All screenshots or captures are 33 megapixels images.

How to shoot 12-bit RAW

The 12-bit RAW is only available on the Samsung S21 ultra; so if you're a user of the Samsung galaxy S21 or S21+ you won't be able to use this feature. For individuals who use the Samsung S21 ultra. 12-bit RAW is a new incredible feature that Samsung added to the ultra in order to boost its camera ability and features.

According to our research, RAW files are actually "digital negatives", what this means is that they do not record digital sharpness or white balance in an image, and this makes the image much more basic and good for photo editing. The 12-bit RAW feature is made for professional photographers, so if you're a professional photographer reading this guide, you should find the 12-bit RAW easy to use.

However, whether professional or not, the 12-bit RAW can be used by anybody as far as you're using the Samsung galaxy S21 ultra and you're following this guide. 12-bit RAW is said to capture more dynamic range which results in well detailed and highlighted images. It's a professional feature, that's why before you can shoot in 12-bit RAW, you have to go to MORE and activate PRO MODE. In PRO MODE, you'll see several settings and this is where your photography skills come in, experiment will be a good start.

Although before you can shoot in RAW mode, you need to activate it in the camera settings, head to the camera settings, select FORMAT AND ADVANCED OPTIONS, then activate RAW copies; this allows your device to take a RAW image and a JPEG image as well.

It is therefore important to note that the raw copies or files take up more space than regular JPEG images, so the feature should be turned off when not in use, unless you like it that way.

Shooting single take 2.0

Single Take, this is another incredible feature that Samsung has made available for its users. The single take feature allows you to capture the best moments, you can use single take to capture wide-angle shots, close-up shots as well as videos.

One amazing thing about the single take feature is that fine tuning the recording time is absolutely doable. In this section, we would be showing you how to take shots using a single take.

Following the steps below, you'll be able to take single take shots;

1.   Launch the gallery application from the app screen of your Samsung S21

2.   Select Single Take from the options menu

3.   Select the shutter button, and then pan the device around to capture best shots and scene clips. Camera automatically captures best shots and clips.

4.   When done, select the thumbnail, you'll find all the images you've taken there.

5.   If you want to view the results, move the icon upwards

6.   To save results individually, choose select then tick the ones you wish to save.

7.   Afterwards, select the arrow icon that's facing downwards.

The single takes AI, captures up to ten different kinds of images and four different kinds of videos, and all these are captured from 3-10 seconds.

All the single take results are saved in the gallery.

CHAPTER TWELVE

How to reset camera app settings

There are sometimes when you'd have tweaked the camera app settings, and it's now feels like trash, too much of modification can make your camera settings stupid and you'll want to reset it to its default settings. That's absolutely what we'll be showing you in this section, using the process below, you should be able to reset your camera settings in no time.

1.   Launch the camera application from the home screen of your Samsung S21

2.   Choose settings, it is located at the top left corner of the camera interface

3.   Select GENERAL

4.   Choose RESET then choose YES

Very short procedure, if you perform the above function, you've successfully reset your camera app settings.

How to use Bokeh

Adding the Bokeh effect to your photos is a good way to use depth of field, the bokeh feature is quite different from the portrait feature. In this section, we'll be showing you how to add Bokeh to your pictures. We've listed the steps required below;

1.   Launch the camera application from the home screen of your Samsung S21

2.   Switch to the rear camera of the device.

3.   Swipe till it gets to Live focus mode

4.   Make sure light comes through from the background before you take a photo

5.   Check the image taken and modify the blurred background

6.   Modify and adjust options then select "tick" to save the photo.

That's all; you've successfully added Bokeh to your picture.

CHAPTER THIRTEEN

How to zoom in and zoom out

This is a basic function and as a photographer you really shouldn't be taught this; however, for some reasons we decided to add this guide in order to make it a complete and well comprehensive guide for beginners as well as professional photographers. In this section, we'll be showing you how to zoom in and zoom out.

Here are the easy steps below:

1.   Launch the camera application from the home screen of your Samsung S21

2.   To zoom in, pinch the camera interface with your two fingers.

3.   Spread the two pinched fingers to zoom out

4.   You can also drag the slider to the left or right to zoom in or out.

How to configure shooting mode

There are different shooting modes in the new Samsung galaxy S21 and as an expert or beginner photography it is advisable that you try out all the modes and master them so as to render them effectively when shooting on a paid service.

How do you arrange or configure shooting modes isn't actually necessary, what's important is trying out these modes.

Here are some incredible shooting modes that are available in the Samsung S21;

1.   **Singe Take:** We've discussed this shooting mode in previous chapters of this book

2.   **HDR+10 mode:** We've also discussed this mode, explaining extensively how it works.

3.   **108MP mode:** This mode is only available for users of the Samsung S21 ultra, if you're using the Samsung S21 or S21+, then you won't be able to use this mode. Activating the 108MP mode isn't difficult at all, in the camera app, just select the 3:4 108MP and that's all, you've enabled 108MP mode and can now take shots with it.

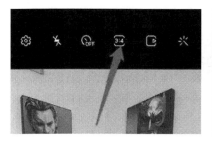 

4.   **Directors View mode:** We'll be showing you how to use this mode and more about it in the coming chapters of this book.

5.   **Panoramas Mode:** This mode is easily accessible; you'll find it in more items.

There are other modes that aren't mentioned above; however, it is important you try out all the modes available in your device.

AR Zone features

AR zone features is what we'd be discussing in this section, AR zone is filled with different AR emojis and AR doodles, In this zone you can select any of the features you prefer and capture fun videos and photos.

Here's how to get to the AR zone features;

1.   Go to the app menu of your Samsung S21 by sliding from down to up on your home screen

2.   Choose the Samsung folder

3.   Select AR zone.

4.   Once in the AR zone application, you'll be able to access all the AR features.

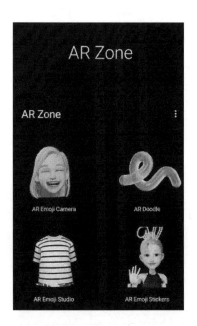

5.   Some of the AR features include;

- **Quick Measure:** Size and distance of the object or subject can be measured hastily.

- **AR Doodle:** This allows you to record videos making them fun by using visual handwritings, drawings on faces and so on.

- **AR Emoji camera:** Build an emoji that looks just like you; you can also take pictures or record videos using My emoji.

- **Deco pic:** Take snapshots and record videos with various stickers.

- **AR Emoji studio:** Build your own My emoji stickers.

CHAPTER FOURTEEN

Computational photography

This may sound new to you, but as a photographer, computational photography is one of the terminologies you should know. In this section, we would be explaining briefly what computational photography is.

What is computational photography?

Computer photography can simply be defined as the use of computer processing abilities in different cameras to manufacture an improved image which will go beyond what the lens and sensor takes up in a single shot.

This computational photography is now available in most smartphones and Samsung galaxy S21 is one of those smartphones that possess enhanced computational photography. Computational photography improves images using different methods and processes, adding depth of field, reducing motion blur and enhancing color and brightness is what computational photography does.

As the level of photography improves drastically in smartphones, computational photography is now one of the most searched keywords online, as every photographer wants to know what computational photography is. In this section, I guess we've shown you and given you insight on what computational photography is.

It is therefore important to note that computational photography brings out the uniqueness and quality of an image.

HP Sprocket

HP sprocket is an application which is available to android users, you can use HP sprocket to edit, print or share your photos.

205

You can download the HP sprocket app from Playstore and use it to edit your photos. To edit photos on the HP sprocket app, simply click on the pencil icon, you can apply filters; add frames, text, stickers and many more. You can also resize and rotate your image using your two fingers to pinch zoom.

Selecting the printer icon prints out your photo. Save photos, you've edited and also print, or share them to loved ones.

Use Photobooth on Hp sprocket; Photobooth allows you to take four photos in a row. After installing the Hp sprocket app, launch it and swipe to Photobooth, select the shutter button to take photobooth images, explore and see how it works.

HP sprocket seems like the best app to use for Photo ID, to use Hp Sprocket for photo ID, use the procedures below:

1.   Launch the Hp sprocket app.

2.   Follow the command for choosing backgrounds, getting rid of accessories and positioning your face or a friend's face.

3.   Select the photo dimensions.

There are other sections you can check out in the Hp sprocket app, sections like Custom stickers and Tile printing, these sections are straightforward and understandable.

Mpow Selfie Stick Tripod

The Mpow selfie stick Tripod is one of the best of its kind, as it has multiple uses, it's beautiful and stress free to use. In this section, we'll be discussing the features and usage of the Mpow selfie stick tripod. The Mpow tripod has adjustable light making your visual world more amazing and embellished. The upgraded tripod stand that the Mpow selfie stick possesses can serve multiple purposes such as; a mobile phone tripod, an action camera tripod and a desktop phone holder. This Tripod can be used with your Samsung galaxy S21, which is why we've included it in this guide.

CHAPTER FIFTEEN

How to use Trash bin

The trash bin is a place where deleted photos and files go to, on your Samsung device, when a file is deleted; it is transferred to the trash bin and kept there for 30 days before it is removed permanently. In this section, we would be showing you how you can restore photos or files that you've deleted but you want them back.

If you mistakenly deleted a file or photo from your Samsung device, do not fret, you can easily get it back just by going to the trash bin and restoring it; however, make sure to make up your mind before 30 days else it would be deleted permanently and there'd be no way to get it back.

There are two places that you can restore from, it's either you're restoring from the Gallery app or you're restoring from the My files app. Don't worry we'll show you how to go about using each of them.

If you mistakenly deleted photos, restoring them from the gallery app is faster, here's how to do it below;

1.   Launch the gallery app from your Samsung galaxy S21 app screen.

2.   To restore already deleted photos, select

3.   Choose **Recycle bin** from the list of options

4.   Choose the photo or video, that you'd like to restore

5.   Then choose   , the image will be restored.

6.   To restore multiple images, tap and hold an image then select the others you wish to restore, then tap on **Restore**

Now if you deleted a document, ringing tone or any file and you wish to restore it, using the "My files app" is the best way. See steps below;

1.   Launch the My files app from your Samsung galaxy S21 app screen.

1.   Select the three dots icon ⋮

2.   Choose recycle bin from the list of options

3.   Tap and hold the file you wish to restore.

4.   Choose restore.

Simple as that, you've successfully learnt how to restore images and files.

Using Galaxy S21 to snap images of the stars

The Samsung galaxy S21 and S21 ultra have been said to be a device that can turn individuals into astrophotographers. Taking pictures of the Milky Way is not an easy thing because you'd need a lot of equipment and photography skills to achieve that feat. However, in this guide, we've decided to bring up this topic in order to teach our readers the simplest way of taking images of the stars. As far as you've got your Samsung galaxy S21, S21+ or ultra, you're one step ahead.

With Samsung's drastic improvement in their camera features, shooting the stars has become the talk of the town as every photography freak wants to try it out, using the pro mode and some other photography skills, you should get a good shot of the milky way. Not to talk much, we'll be going straight to the steps on how to shoot images of the stars using your Samsung galaxy S21.

When going for a night capture, you should go when the moon isn't up, that is, a moonless night, this way you get a better view of the Milky Way. And you must take along with you a backup phone battery and also a rechargeable flashlight.

Follow the procedures below;

1.	On getting there, the first thing you should do is to set up your equipment.

2.　To shoot the stars, you need a tripod to help hold your device so as to avoid shaking, you'd also need a remote shutter or timed shutter, because you'll need to make the camera very stagnant so it'd be able to absorb light.

3.　The Samsung camera isn't built for shooting the stars, so you'd have to do some settings to achieve this feat, use pro mode, you can find that in More items if you swipe down the different modes available on the camera app. Also make sure your camera is in manual mode not automatic, so you have control over everything.

4.　Modify and adjust shutter speed, use a slow shutter speed, because your shutter speed needs to be open for a little while in order for it to take in light for the capture. With this, you'd capture even star trails.

5.　Modify and adjust the white balance color, white balance reduces and increases the temperature of the camera, this means objects that seem white in your eye will actually display as white when the photo is ready. According to our research, 4500 or less would be suitable for astrophotography.

6.   Make your ISO sensitivity right; modify your ISO settings as it has a great impact on the image brightness, the higher the ISO the brighter your images. However, it isn't advisable to use too much ISO as it may affect and ruin the picture.

7.   We also discussed in this guide how to save files in RAW, so make sure you've switched to RAW before shooting the stars.

CHAPTER SIXTEEN

Ways to improve photography in Samsung Galaxy S21

All what we've taught you in this guide are actually the ways that you require in improving your Photography using the Samsung galaxy S21. However, we just intend to give you a brief on how you can up your photography game.

Arrange the modes at the bottom of your camera interface to the way you want it, this is very important and will make you look like a professional when taking photographs, we omitted this when we were discussing *How to configure shooting modes*. Arranging your shooting modes is one of the best ways to improve your photography as it gives you ease and less stress, so if you know the modes you use regularly or like best, you can arrange them one after the other on the bottom of your camera interface.

To arrange the shooting modes on your camera interface, here's what you need to do; select More on the end of the modes list. Then drag any mode in the More list into the bottom tray, to take away a mode you don't want, drag it to the tray, do this to edit and rearrange your shooting modes, then choose save when you're done.

After adjusting and rearranging your shooting modes, it'll be easy for you to capture beautiful moments with your Samsung S21.

Another way of improving your photography is by trying out new tips and tricks, trying out all the modes, tweaking stuff and exploring the camera application.

About director's view on GALAXY S21

The director's view is one of the shooting modes available in the Samsung galaxy S21, in the previous chapter of this guide; we told you that we'd be talking extensively on this subject. Now here we are, in this section, we'll discuss briefly about the director's view mode and how to activate it.

As the name implies the Director's view mode allows you to seamlessly use both the front and rear camera when recording a video, this mode makes you the director, you can work with both the rear and front camera simultaneously making your videos look like a directed film recording. Isn't that incredible? This mode is a very useful one for individuals who uses both cameras to record videos.

Activating the director's view mode is not something difficult, it's just a mode you pick from the shooting modes, here's how to activate it below;

1.	Launch your camera app from your Samsung galaxy S21 home screen.

2.	Choose more from the ribbon below, it may be written as More items.

3.	Select Director's view mode.

4.	Now start shooting that video.

CONCLUSION

In this guide we've talked about everything that can make you become a professional Samsung S21 photographer, after reading this guide completely, it'll be very easy for you to capture perfect and mind blowing images. Readers are advised to go through each section carefully to grasp the teachings and steps explained in them.

All the steps that we've outlined in this guide have been tested specifically so there's nothing wrong in any of the steps, if you don't understand a step, read it again for better assimilation. If you're a photography freak, you'll learn dozens of new things in this guide, and from a freak you'd become an export in mobile photography.

For users to understand and completely assimilate, we've decided to use simplest English with less grammar, anything you find hard to understand might be a term in photography which I'm sure we explained extensively in the guide. Each section tells you what you'll learn before you start reading, so you'd have an objective before you read a section.

Detailed images have been placed in specific places for more in-depth understanding of what the writer is trying to portray. This guide was prepared for Samsung S21 users who would love to know about how the Samsung S21 camera works, nevertheless, amateur and beginners mobile photographers would gain a lot from the guide.

ABOUT THE AUTHOR

Curtis Campbell is an intelligent and innovative computer scientist with experience in software engineering. As a renowned technology expert, his passion for capturing still photos and motion pictures has led him into photography and videography, which he is doing with excellence. Curtis has produced several tutorials on different topics. As a researcher and a prolific writer with proficiency in handling tech products, he learned different approaches to managing issues on the internet and other applications.

Samsung Galaxy S21 Camera Guide

Made in United States
Troutdale, OR
07/20/2023

11438170R00133